STRANGERS

&

PILGRIMS

SAINT JULIAN PRESS

POETRY

ALSO BY ALFRED. K. LAMOTTE

Wounded Bud: Poems for Meditation
(2013, Saint Julian Press)

Savor Eternity One Moment at a Time
(2015, Saint Julian Press)

The Nectar of This Breath
(2022, Saint Julian Press)

Shimmering Birthless: A Confluence of Verse and Image
(2015, co-author with artist/publisher Rashani Réa)

Fire of Darkness: What Burned Me Away Completely, I Became
(2019, co-author with artist/publisher Rashani Réa)

Nameless: Rashani Réa and Six Contemporary Poets
(2021, co-author with artist/publisher Rashani Réa)

Praise for Strangers & Pilgrims

"Oh, these poems, how they move me, fragrant as they are with wonder, fear, embodiment, love, and sacred longing. Each page is an invitation to "awaken the one you already are." I've long loved Alfred K. LaMotte's work, and with this collection, I fall even more deeply in love with life, with truth, with great teachers, and with "the miraculous wings of the ordinary." After just ten minutes of reading *Strangers and Pilgrims*, I feel more human, more spacious, more at home, more light."

~Rosemerry Wahtola Trommer
All the Honey & Host of *The Poetic Path (Ritual App)*

"I deeply admire Alfred K. LaMotte as a person and poet. The source he taps is a clear living spring of divine solace and inspired grace. Each book he creates seems to introduce the world to a new species of beauty. The energy in his words is resuscitation. Each poem is an oasis. Thank God for poets like him."

~Chelan Harkin
Susceptible to Light and *Bouquet of Stars*

"Alfred K. LaMotte is a passionate seeker, a modern mystic in whose wild and tender heart springs devotion for the Sacred Feminine. He gives voice to the paradoxes of living embodied spirituality. In the prophetic poetic tradition of Rumi and Hafiz, he expresses an unfettered yearning for union with the Divine. His poems pulse with sparkling traces of his search for a fuller humanity, in the hope that they might kindle in you the courage to follow your own path and claim your inner treasure."

~Kayleen Asbo, Ph.D.
Mary Magdalene Scholar & Pilgrimage Leader
Founder of Mythica Community

"Alfred LaMotte's poetry is to the human soul what breath is to the physical body!"

~Rashani Réa
Beyond Brokenness and *Beneath All Appearances: An Unwavering Peace*

"I want to pull these poems around me so they might infuse my dreams. I want to hold them like a lens to better see the stars. Alfred LaMotte is such a wise yet wonder-filled writer!"

~Laura Grace Weldon
Author of *Portals*
Braided Way Magazine - Editor
2019 Ohio Poet of the Year

"The world often estranges us from our hearts and distracts us with theatre and puppetry. But when I slow down, breathe, and read these poems with the respect they deserve, the words ring so strong they pull me back to my heart. These poems remind us why we are here: to deliberately choose divine Presence in every moment. They make the pain of living a wholehearted, spiritual, authentic life more bearable, reminding me that I am not alone. This brings solace in a way that nothing else can. Thank you for these sacred words and for making a space where we can all breathe together."

~Abby Wynne
The Inner Compass Trilogy

"Fred is among the most prolific poets whose writings have touched and inspired me for many years. His poems are not dry intellectual discourses. They are medicine for the troubled world. They taste like spring water in the desert. The depth and simplicity from where his words spill wake us up and remove all our unnecessary worries and fear. Please come and rest inside the vastness of his offering!"

~Guthema Roba
Song of Silence: Sacred Poems for Healing and Awakening

STRANGERS & PILGRIMS

Poems

by

Alfred K. LaMotte

SAINT JULIAN PRESS
HOUSTON

Published by
SAINT JULIAN PRESS, Inc.
2053 Cortlandt, Suite 200
Houston, Texas 77008

www.saintjulianpress.com

ISBN-13: 978-1-955194-21-1
Library of Congress Control Number: 2023944695

Cover Art Credit: *Indwelling Peace*
Sue Ellen Parkinson
http://www.sueellenparkinson.com/

TO MY PATIENT AND EVER-SUPPORTIVE WIFE, ANNA.
AND TO MY GUIDE, MARY MAGDALENE, WHOSE BREATH
OF GRACE INSPIRES THESE POEMS.

CONTENTS

INTRODUCTION

The longing of the pilgrim and the joy of union are not two paths, but one. This apparent contradiction is the fuel of awakening. Some of these poems reflect Advaita, "nonduality." Others reflect Bhakti, "yearning for the Beloved." The first poem embraces fear and helplessness at our present condition on earth; the rest respond to that despair. Another paradox: some poems poke fun at the New Age spiritual marketplace, which all too glibly sells nonduality like a plastic rose, instantly attainted. Yet other poems revere the Guru, the real one, that rare Friend who awakens the radiance of God in the heart's dark night, through the gift of meditation.

This book is devoted to Mary Magdalene, who "lifts us up into our fallenness." The Magdalene poems are not in one section, but sewn like seeds throughout the book. For me, she is the feminine consort of Christ: they are two poles of the same consciousness. She embodies the Holy Spirit, the breath of the Divine. She is what Yoga tradition calls *Shakti*, the feminine power of God.

Mary Magdalene works not through what is perfect, but what is broken, bewildered and estranged. In the cover painting by Sue Ellen Parkinson, Mary stands on the shore of southern France where waves of destiny tossed her rudderless boat. According to popular tradition, she awakened Christ Consciousness in the West. Meditating in a cave among the hills of Province, she radiated divine love to the primitive continent of Europe. Now pilgrims gather there from all over the world. While exploring Medieval pilgrimage routes in 1972, I met her there in prayer, innocently, with no knowledge of her journey to Europe. She became my "Anam Cara," my soul friend. For me, she personifies the paradox: yearning and union are entwined, one vine.

Now let me share a secret, hinted often in these poems. The portals to heaven are in the body. In native Hawaiian, Laniakea means "immense heaven." Astronomers chose this name for the supercluster of 100,000 galaxies where our Milky Way is but a tiny dot. Within this spark swarm 300 billion stars, including our sun, a golden dust-mote sustaining the earth and planets. In all this radiance, perhaps you feel so small. But who is aware of that abyss surrounding the edges of time? You are. Even as you hear these words, do you not visualize those galaxies, floating in unbounded silence? Of course you do. Is your awareness not the very space of which you are aware? Therefore, the whole cosmos happens in your consciousness.

Close your eyes, breathe in. Feel attention rising up your spine like amrita, like sap, all the way to the top of your skull, nourishing the hollows in your flesh. Rest in your fontanelle, that spot so tender at infancy, before the bone gates closed to shut out the Infinite. Let the grace of inhalation soften your crown again. Gentleness is your birthright. A thousand angels come and go with the rising and falling of your breath.

As you exhale, let awakened awareness soak like gentle mist through your body, down to the sacrum, out through the toes, into the earth. Allow this breath of wonder to continue, refreshing every cell. When you are ready, feel her lips touch the top of your skull: She who was at play with the Creator in the beginning of time (Proverbs 8:30). Call her Shakti, Shekinah, the Magdalene, or Qi. She appears in every wisdom tradition. The one who "whirled the stars into their chalices" has come to dwell in your body as this breath.

When She touches your nape, don't you scent her fragrance? When her nectar drips down the mala beads of your vertebrae, don't you taste the vintage of the stars? You yearn for this, don't you? And in this very yearning is her presence, her bouquet. Here is the mystery of the Magdalene: the longing of strangers and pilgrims contains what it longs for. Be still. Let your stillness ferment into love, greening the earth. Are we not all, "one breath in eight billion bodies?"

I offer these poems not to change you, but to awaken the one you already are. I bequeath them to many mouths: the cocoon, the wine skin, the space between tears, the silent trough between thoughts, the lips that would cry like wind in the sea of anger and remorse, if they knew how; the mouth of a sparrow who sings among olive branches in the desert where your soul dwells, lonely and unique; the mouth of the rose that grows among thorns by the ocean in a ruined abbey.

I bequeath them to the parted lips of one just dead, and the lips of evening where the sun melts, a final drop of communion fire in the quietness between earth and sky. I sow these poems in your lips, friend, in your wound, in your well, planting them where you are most vulnerable, the place our bruises touch, where we have both fallen, where our mouths meet, searching for the Word.

There is a furrow between the seasons. No season is not the season of Grace. Perhaps you cannot tell if this be Winter or Spring, Summer's end or Autumn's beginning. The sacrament of life on earth is impermanence. Yet eternity comes to dwell here. Let these poems be brief kisses on the mouth of Ever, in the frail brown body of the word, Everchanging.

Alfred K. LaMotte
July 22, 2023

"And they confessed that they were strangers and pilgrims on the earth."

~Hebrews 11:13

STRANGERS

et

PILGRIMS

SCARY

The world is scary.
I'm scared.
That's the truth.
How about you?
The world is in chaos
and I refuse to pretend
that I know what to do.
Do you hear me?
I'm scared
and I don't know.
Yet when I tell
the Truth, a sacred
white buffalo
wanders into my heart
and I feel a peace
the world cannot give
or take away.
Do you hear me?
Perhaps this is what
we can all do together:
Be scared.
Don't know.
Tell the truth.

ON CERTAIN AFTERNOONS

On certain afternoons
   the radiance of things
just as they are, requires
     no politics, no ideology.
First it rains,
   then the sun comes out,
     the warming and cooling
of the globe, the updraft
   and downfall of my breathing.
Both Winter and Summer
   I am free, no more important
     than a morning glory.
Most of my DNA
   I share with a mouse,
     infinitude with a gnat.
Endangered herds stampede
   through the wounded valleys
     of my marrow,
I protect vast swaths
   of rain forest
      with a single exhalation.
I'm certain that the merest weed
   in its stillness is awake,
     a blossoming black-eyed-susan.
Rooted in listening, I also flower
   with no seed of thought.
     The soil is my Being.
     Wonder is the musk of my heart.
      May my fragrance expand
      beyond all gardens.
Come, you lovers of late Spring,
     the gates are never closed.
The rain-disheveled azalea
   will not begrudge your insouciance,
     nor the rose your burning fingers.
Let each dare to whisper
   in your own tongue,
     "Smell me, I am wild!"

PLUMFALL

True lovers abandon
this word, love.
It is no substitute
for a thud of plums
in the mist before dawn,
or the first apple
thumping sweetly into the birdbath
at midnight.
True lovers feel
the passion of Christ
in the ripening
of a huckleberry.
They hear each verse
of the holy Qu'ran
in a thrush's throat,
and the Song of Solomon
in the pine breeze,
the elegiac coyote,
the rain that whispers all night,
"Be breathed."
In the morning
they are intoxicated
by the feral bouquet
of their own nakedness.
True lovers know that
the Mysteries
can never be named:
a ball of goat's fur tangled in lupine,
a blue moth disguising her wings
as an alpine aster,
taste of honeysuckle, grace
of a whole afternoon without
naming the world: no Word
but what things are.

ASHORE

"Not everyone who wanders is lost." ~J.R.R. Tolkein

The wilderness invites
your whirling heart,
rudderless, eddied, spun
by an incoming tide,
entangled in a chaos
of weed and beach foam,
still beaten by the breath
of your beloved,
keeping his promise
to the urchin and hermit crab.
Now meander inland,
until you're good and lost
like Jesus,
then take off your shoes
and call it home.
With every step, the earth
says "welcome."
You never even get close
to where you were going.
The only consolation
is to throw away your map
and start dancing in your
olive dark body
right where you are.
Open your palms toward sunset.
Pray without naming the stars
that arrive one by one
like honored guests, bending
to touch your bare feet.
After all, aren't you made
from their curved journeys of light?
Dust is your sacrament now.
Wiggle your toes in thanksgiving.
Linger, but do not stay.
Be a wanderer.

SHIFT

The Shift is not a happening
in time.
Not something you need
to wait for.
The Shift is a blessed
and perpetual fall
from the chatter in your brain
to heart-hollowed quietness;
from the abstract to the local,
swollen repose
of a snow-bound crocus,
racket of flycatchers
over thawed bog water,
improbable worlds condensed
into pearls of the ordinary
like the sweat
of sweetness on a plum.
The Shift could be
a stinging caress
of moist burnt-umber soil
on your barefoot soles.
Or the fondle of this breath
kindling a flame of Presence
through the gray mirage
of your exhausted story.
Now why don't you
soften your belly.
Why don't you shift
into the place where you are,
relishing the only certain
warmth there is,
your body.

TEMPLE IN THE VALLEY

Just below the left ventricle
and just above the solar plexus
is a temple in the valley
of breathing.
And here, two fingers' width
in front of your chest
to be precise, is a flame
that does not burn
but gives unfiltered sweetness,
a quiver of spun fiber
for arrows of starlight.
Both triangles point here
from above and below,
the hollow hexagram
of Presence.
All equations are balanced
by the in-breath
that holds this space.
The constellations, those beasts
of silence, gather here
to drink from the spring
which Jesus called a well
of everlasting life, and Milarepa
the bee-drowning jewel
at the center of the lotus,
a bafflement of proportions
that drive mathematicians
mad in search of beauty.
Perhaps the name of Krishna
will draw you here, perhaps
the name of Christ, or the secret
name of the Goddess, born
on a vapor of surrender.
But really, you won't comprehend
this radiance at all, until
you gaze upon the face
of the Friend in the mirror
of your own heart.

PRONOUNS

Let all your pronouns
dissolve in *Thou*.
You are not a gender
or a tribe,
a nation or a race.
You are the one
who was born to gaze
into my face,
as I was born
to gaze into yours.
Our religion
is a broken heart,
spilling light
out of darkness.
We meet in the smell
of food,
giving thanks
to the smallest creatures,
the bee, the seed,
the raindrop,
learning from a withered
Autumn sunflower
how to scatter a thousand
Summer mornings.

SHAMAN BABY

So you want to be a certified
Machu Picchu Shaman?
But you're already there.
You danced the twelve constellations, tumbling
through the amniotic intergalactic womb.
You were baptized in the sweat lodge of the birth canal,
your microbiome bubbling with talismans.
Initiation was your first breath.

Each morning in your crib,
a grasshopper, serpent, peacock, frog,
you performed the total phylogenic sequence of asanas,
and embodied eons, your wrists and fingers playing
Buddhic mudras, your throat a bone rattle,
belly a drum, lips gurgling incantations to invoke
your animal familiars, a spaniel, a tabby cat,
a parakeet named Sanchez.
Your burbles and farts were tantric bija mantras filled
with God's Word: *Hum! Phwat! Hri! Gah!*
Creation through baby talk.

Your epithelium the robe of the Deer Priest.
Wingéd jaguars in the rain forest of your cerebellum.
Hidden in the leaves of your medulla, a sepulcher
containing your medicine bundle, the amygdala.
And in the ancient well of your pineal gland,
a turquoise ayahuaska toad, who spat crystal wisdom
into your forehead, star-juice down your backbone.
Distant suns fell through the soft spot in your skull
like rebel angels.

Fiery polypeptide tendrils in your solar plexus
streamed beyond your edgeless flesh.
Neurons rooted through your naked toes,
entwining with mycelium.
Your diaphragm a lyre of gut strings,
resonant with hummingbird thunder.
Dust, fire, water, air, offered to the jungle God,
Viracocha, through the burning sage smoke
of your original amazement....

Shaman: "one who sees in the dark."
The stars are only beautiful
because the night around them is so deep.
Even now you are that child
who beholds the full moon of beauty
ascending in the opal sky
between your eyebrows.

As young this day you are as all
the celestial bodies whose fire
has not yet reached into your flesh.
Here, in your lungs, where
rising touches falling,
there is a gateway to marvelous worlds.
What flowers in that furrow is the kiss
of earth and heaven.

Your senses do not consume the world,
they suffuse it, nostrils, ears, eyes, tongue
irradiating creation with a Self.
You bless by beholding.
Now take, no, receive this breath.

Even now you might perambulate
those terrible holy flowers,
the sacrum, navel, throat and crown.
Even now you might follow
the winding way with a pilgrim goddess
who walks with you through Eden again
in the cool of the evening,
placing the lost rib back in your side,
where it blossoms.

HALF-VEILED

Beauty is more lovely
half-veiled.
Don't give it all away.
Let there be a portion of your silence
that falls into deeper silence.
Be like the new moon
pulling on a garden from within.
The mystery of an azure moth
disappearing on blue chicory,
seen only by one whose
gaze has been polished by waiting.
Cocoon your revelation.
This is the way of wings.
Astonishing colors begin
with starlight in dew
on lilac leaves at midnight.
Discretion of a cloud
reflected on a forest pond,
there, and not there.
The age of restraint,
the discipline of intimacy,
beginning in our eyes, my love,
my sister, pilgrim friend,
as we bend blind beams
of wanting into the rainbow
of a subtler body, chiaroscuro
of prudence and delight.
Let there be a renaissance
of veils, fashioning our fierce
eternal fire into the sweetness
of this moment on earth.
Tempered, let me touch
the bright erotic darkness
of your soul.

PLUNGE

Stars have a secret.
They are always falling
into orbits of glory.
They do not attempt to fly.
Darkness is their wing.
If you don't believe me,
you're still trying not to fall.
Plunge more deeply
into the womb of night
and you will draw very near
to the radiance
of your Birth.
Call it the hollow
that runs up your spine,
the axis through the nest
of all that whirls.
Call it uncreated light,
the dawn descending
from the heart of Andromeda,
holding in tiny cups
the coming Spring,
seeds of a new creation,
sun-curved embryos
gazing into their own hands,
buds unclenching their pollen,
shaping their dreams on the tip
of a stamen.
Or say the secret is
these twin beams of infinity
gazing through all centers
from the mirror of your face
into the mirror of mine,
until they collide in
the kiss, the catastrophe
that is everywhere.

HOW WILL YOU KNOW HER?

Between your heartbeats is a garden,
the place where Magdalene and Jesus touch.
She thinks he is the gardener. He thinks she is
God's breath, caressing his chest. She is.

Between your heartbeats is a garden,
the wilderness where Israel meets Wisdom,
the Sabbath Queen who sings of loss.
How could they make love in the desert?
They pitch a tent of animal skins, and it becomes
a holy pavilion of gathered silences.

Between your heartbeats is a garden
where village girls dance with the Prince of Herdsmen.
Each maiden is his flute, but only one can be his Song.
She who wears your inhalation as her wedding gown
has come to wound you in the pulse of your throat.
How will you know her? By what signs
will you prove that she is your Betrothed?

Dear friend, your emptiness turns indigo,
fragrant as jasmine, your numb places overflow
like awakened breasts. And this smoldering
in the soul is your body. When you breathe
through the bruise in your crown, your bones
fill up with orphaned lightning. When your heart beats,
one grail breaks against another, mingling tinctures
of birth and death. You become a vineyard, edges
un-gleaned, where wandering pilgrims eat their fill.

All night a Goddess presses her kiss of solitude
between your eyes, a dreamless throbbing pearl.
The unwavering flame on the wick of your spine
consumes the oil of wonder, whose scent is love.
In the darkest hour you cease to ask for light,
because the midnight stillness under your breastbone
has become a maelstrom of stars. And the dignity
of this inhalation, how it gently places the spirit
in each cell of your flesh, is your Lover's secret name.

WINGS

All the miracles
you do not notice
this summer morning
fly back to their Creator
on disappointed wings,
amber-gold salmon berry,
liquid amethyst on
the lip of a maidenhair fern,
crocosmia, this
tooth of Lucifer;
while all the miracles
that you behold
fold their wings to settle
in the commonplace.
"Let there be light"
is not a Word from
the beginning, but a shout
in the language of now.
Creation remains
unfinished, friend,
without the beams
of your attention.
Have you never grown
still enough to hear
the first commandment?
"Thou shalt notice the toadstool,
the forget-me-not, a web
of dew, a pebble."
You are here to perceive
the miraculous wings
of the ordinary.
Your astonishment
completes the design.

ALCHEMY OF ANGER

Anger is meat
too gamey for the mind.
Consume it with your body.
With the fierce massage
of the faintest breath,
your wrath bursts into blossom
through the solar plexus,
pulses in the forehead,
bubbles up your marrow,
heating your ancestors'
bone broth to keep
the bowels of Winter warm.
Feel it without resistance.
No label, no brand, not
even the word, "anger."
Taste the piquant fire.
Neither right nor wrong,
anger just is.
Delicious.
It shall be a panther
who glides down to the
waterhole in your desert.
It shall be a coral snake
who squeezes
like a feral rainbow
out of your old skin.
Your raven anger shall rise
on tawny wings altered
scarlet and gold by dawn,
never returning to her gray
nest of broken sticks
and brittle stories.
Cluster your tongues
of ire into an amethyst
of pure attention,
then slip it on the ring
finger of your most beloved
enemy.

PLEIN-AIRE

"A certain blue enters your soul." ~Matisse

Use azure
and aquamarine discreetly,
as nature does,
not her most
common colors,
but the tones she reserves
for caesuras, vanishing
horizons, the depth
of forest pools,
abyss of a morning glory,
or a finch's egg
whose curve somehow
contains the sky
over Lemnos in June,
the color of
stillness in the mind
between thoughts,
and when we gaze
into each other's faces,
where we go,
where we come
to rest,
the purest blue.

ISHQ ALLAH

You taught me your hunger language. Ishq Allah Ma'bud Allah!
"The Lord is love, lover, and beloved."

Now I know God's native tongue, though my grammar is confused.
The pronouns bewilder me, because I have fallen into the flower
of your wound, whose petals are Mine, Yours, His, Hers, Ours.

It is a groundless falling, a ravenous exchange of lips and silences,
gazes of Otherness in a single eye: Ishq Allah Ma'bud Allah!

All that matters is the wave nature of the moon, the secret kiss of the bee
in the pistil of the hyacinth. All that matters is the sexual caress of
listener and stillness, the tremor of silence where the music is conceived.

The blue note in your flute has become a sky, where I taste the death
of distances. In the star-swirled center of my forehead, I drown your
dark embryo.

You take rebirth as a drop in my eye, and I as a drop in yours.
Healing, like a bellows, is the gift of hollowness.

Is your desert night above me, or inside? Your constellations arrange
themselves in the shape of a hand over my slumbering face. You flow in,
I flow out, ebbing into the diamond blackness that is always awake.

Some imagine moons and suns to be out above. But they are my tears,
caught in the silken web of your longing for me.

Inhalation is the pilgrimage to a temple nearer than stillness.
Exhalation carries us across the void. One stirs the buried seed,
the other releases sap, bathing the earth in bittersweet prayer.

I lacerate my lungs with this invitation: fill me, empty me,
drown me in the waves of your Name. Ishq Allah Ma'bud Allah!

O stranger, pilgrim, seeker of lethal cleansing transformations,
wield your breath wisely, for it is a burning sword of love.

SHATTER

Now tell me, is there
a deeper beauty
than the color
of silence?
Breathing in,
breathing out,
I am burnishing
the mirror in my chest
that I might see
the amethyst in the rose
of your countenance,
so clearly, so clearly,
that it shatters
the difference
between us.

TAKE OFF YOUR SHOES

Go outside. Take off your shoes.
Breathe sunlight through your crown,
the tender spot where the bones
of your story never closed.
Feel honey trickle down your vertebrae.

A ray of violet bathes your crinkled brow,
transmuting anger into joyous useful fury.
Caress your throat with rays of
song-bird grief-healing yellow.
Soften your clenched heart-bud
in a glow of forest green.

Unfurl one thousand petals in your breast,
each shaped like a perfect wound.
Disentangled by a fragrant breeze,
the knotted thorns in your throat release
their scarlet berries.
Your breath-whisper is the name
of the Goddess.
Notice the golden dahlia that was already there,
pollenated by your microbes.

What's this, fermenting
in the cauldron of your loins?
Your weary disappointment, changed
into a purple vintage bursting up
through the *sushumna*, a rosary of prisms.
From the soles of your feet, breathe
shattered sunbeams.

Now that you know your body is made
from quantum sparks of astonishment,
give birth to the rainbow.
The surrendered have no choice.
For you, white light is not enough.

Here is a holier, more feral secret.
The arc of healing does not shower
down from the sky, it gushes
upward from dust.

Bear a burnt-umber wheat-toned rainbow
percolated out of compost, amber-glow
of splintered bone, afterbirth
of mushroom spores, bacterial chant
of the earthworm.

Give birth to the piebald
treasures of the decomposed.
Breathe in where you once breathed out,
through your sacrum, through your soles,
inhaling the truffled energies
of your grandmother's marrow,
muddy diastole of crystalline detritus.

Glorify the loam! Gather the relics!
Tiny slivers of your first ancestor's femur,
still warm with embered sacrifice.
Now fling these swirling ashes into night.
They are the stars.

HUM

*"Adau Bhagavan shabda rasahi: In the beginning, the Lord created
the universe through a stream of sound." ~Vedic text*

Om is too stuffy, just Hum like a bee, Humming the prayer that created the
cosmos out of silence. It will strengthen your immune system. A gentle Hum
stimulates your vagus nerve, this tree of life in the center of the garden of
your body, this burning bush of neurological fire that Moses saw in the
Cloud of Unknowing on Mount Horeb, from whose flames the voice of the
Formless resonated ten Sefiroth, world-shaping angels, usually mistaken as
"commandments" by un-humming intellectuals trapped in the fruitless
tangle of opposites, which is that other arbor, tree of the knowledge of good
and evil, male and female, black and white. Forget your opposite a little
while, just Hum through your heart and let Humming become the holy
name, the river of sound that sang the galaxies into matter anti-matter and
it doesn't matter from the black hole of womb-silence. Hum the song of
Brahmari the bee Goddess, buzzing through the cranial hive, taming your
feral hypothalamus, opening the reptilian amaretto cask of your amygdala.
Light your pituitary chandelier in the ballroom of the medulla, polishing
your pineal pearl with arrows of Shakti that dart through the eye in your
forehead. Let all your neurons, every cell, make golden honey of the Hum,
dripping down the back of your throat to the subterranean temple in your
ribs, flowing into the grail on the altar of your sternum. So Hum stars
through your belly. So Hum sap through your cervix. Humyoni Humballs
Hum burning seeds of moonlight stored up against time in chthonic caverns
where the unborn suns sleep. Hum.

DISCIPLINE

This is my spiritual discipline.
To act my age,
not one moment old.
To give myself permission to eat
whatever is delicious.
To fall in love with butter again,
warm blueberry pie.
I know that you can smell this.
If humans were created to abstain,
our mothers and fathers would
never have conceived us.
This is my spiritual discipline.
I vow to dance with the perfect stranger,
confuse left and right, outgrow the tribe,
stay vigilant until I hear
the inconceivable concerto
of a white-throated sparrow.
I vow to make one sip last forever.
I vow never to need to explain.
I will wander very gently
over the earth, sauntering nowhere
like a lost pilgrim.
And every morning, I will
breathe away the dream,
glancing inward, smiling
at the radiant looking glass
in the center of my old reptilian brain.
Then I will blamelessly go forth
to embrace my seven billion lovers,
satisfying each with a feast of light,
and a taste of wine
from my jug of folly.

ODE TO HONEYSUCKLE

Even before I wake,
 you are trembling
in summer silence.
 When your name
 softens my heart,
the angry world seems
 to bow
 toward some mysterious
 droplet
 in its own blossom,
 forgetting who to blame.
The sign that you have
 called me is
a tiny broken stamen
 dyeing the whole sky
 with sweetness.
Only you and I are
 insignificant enough
 to understand this.
Our secret befuddles
 the important ones.
The distance between us
 is less than
 a bee's proboscis.
Better than oneness
 is the veil of love.
 I hold you on my tongue.

THE FLAME INSIDE

If the flame inside you
is nothing but anger,
you haven't really begun
to burn.
Rage is just kindling.
Transmute it into
fiercer sweeter fire,
not by struggle and resistance,
nor by gathering
blood-red grief poppies
with their motherload
of dreams for the dying,
but a plunge beyond hope,
a Way that bursts open
when you water it
with loss.
Let your falling body
strike a spark against
the very darkness.
Meteors do this in
the beauty of annihilation.
Songs, when they are over,
do it in silence.
Prayers do it in
ameen, ameen.
And your eyes,
gazing into mine.

I FELL DOWN

I've committed countless sins.
Fireflies over a hayfield
just before dawn.
Tea candles at noon
on the veranda.
Milkweed in a land breeze
over the ocean.
Here's the secret, God
has no interest in our guilt.
I've abandoned penance
and forgiveness.
My heart is the sun
in an empty sky
whose morning outshines
every circumstance
as honey overflows a comb.
My stupefaction governs
all the planets and stars.
When a dandelion is
thoroughly withered and dry,
the frailest sigh blows all
her silver threads away.
So I fall down and sing to ladybugs.
I whisper to grass, "Walk on me!"
Ancient grapes of pain take root,
entwining in my chromosomes,
yet they burst sweetly on my tongue
today! O thirsty pilgrim,
sip the wine of Presence.
Let your gratitude bring peace
upon all this green and holy confusion.
For one world only exists,
the great circle of our breathing.

SEASON BETWEEN

Drop the veil of hope and wanting.
Watch the sun pluck harps of frost
fretted between oak leaves.
Are you not surrounded by wise
ancient beings of immense stature:
cedars, stones, Scarlet Elf Cups,
fieldmice braving the cold?
You hear the chime of stars
in sparkling awareness.
Call it a moment of grace if you like,
but grace is all there is here,
where things are anointed by no-thing,
each creature by subnuclear crystals
of holographic dew,
softer and softer miracles,
dissolving into whispers
of the Name.
And really, isn't it true
that love overflows
the rim of a dust mote?
O mind, plunge naked
into the sacrament of ordinary time,
a season between epiphanies,
where a fiercer listening will arise
within silence itself, and you become
fresh water in an abandoned well.
One breath bows to another.
You remember how to stand here
surrounded by green, to be amazed,
then how to walk.

MOLLUSK

In a mollusk of prayer, yearning chafes the sandy grit of "I" into a pearl.
That is why your pronoun must not be cast out. The motion of the tides
will turn it into something beautiful.

Pain does not redeem us, but the crystal hollow we allow around the
wound. You could become a shell of forgiveness, crush bone to jewel,
marinate in grief salt, let in the moon.

The presence of Our Lady in this inhalation would confuse you if your
flesh had not suffered love's secret. Longing melts edges, barnacles the
formless with gems, churns emptiness into froth.

Fold in lemony stars, mountains, spice forests, terrifying mushrooms.
Then behold the shivering kelp-tangled goddess who stands on the shore,
her gaze refracted through your vast green shadow.

She wonders what lives down here among crustacean silences. You answer
with your final exhalation, a rosary of bubbles, "No one who still has a
name and does not weep, can sip from this savory grail."

She asks why the world is spun so wondrous strange. How your soul
became a vacant swirling eddy, captured by the gravity of blackness.

Why night is swallowed up inside you, like an absence full of diamonds.
Why, at birth, you received an unfathomable touch from the Beloved,
here, in your lungs.

She wants to know whose gentle glance might finally open the tomb,
the well of tears, your mollusk of prayer. You tell her: "Only the morning
star, and the breath of the Beloved, could unseal my heart tonight."

NEVER AGAIN

Never again let it be said, "I am not
this body." Just as your breath
is more than air, so your pulp
is more than what you eat and drink.
She who whirled the stars into their chalices,
churning the cream of darkness
in the cauldron of the Milky Way,
has mantled her Spirit in your tears.
She bends the horizons of dawn and evening
into arcs of praise on your half-parted lips.
And if this breath is her garment,
what is her nakedness if not the fire
that spills from your forehead to your loins?
Kundalini kisses you like this,
revealing the night that has no opposite.
In the cavern of that kiss, it's not
what her name means, but its reverberation
that quickens your sap, thrills your toes,
sprouting dendrites into succulent mire.
A hummingbird murmuring Torah.
The Pleiades entangled in an earthworm.
Tantric mandalas in tree rings.
Her eponym the seed that Jesus drops
in your flesh furrow, unfathomable.
The whole golden vineyard contained
in that tiny spore, clusters of suns
already tipsy on the vine.
She's what first light does to a warbler's throat,
the tremor in your marrow-fat,
your hollow bones her pan pipe perhaps,
a scent of seven caresses up your spine.
Feel the ocean of silence in your belly,
where She walks on moonlight over
rippling waters, offering her luscious
bija like a basket of figs. Friend,
all that ripens is made of that sound.

HOW APRIL COMES

Outside the window
in the branches of your spine,
on a long black twig still cold
with night dew,
plum blossoms silently
burst open.

When you can see things
that happen within you
out there,
and things that happen out there
within you,
then you know how a
breath of wonder
pries open the tomb.

How a savior walks
barefoot through
the disheveled garden,
his voice whispering
"Mary"
almost like a prayer.

How the woman cries
"Rabboni!"
and drops her weighty
urn of tears,
shattering the darkness.
How April comes,
and all the juices
in these earthen jars
turn to wine.

SOFTEN

Merely by resting in your heart
you soften one thousand miles
of space around you.
Those who come near
feel the touch of wild cotton,
the radiance of seven pearls
threaded on a sunbeam.
Their souls begin to orbit your belly button.
They enter your invisible
garden of Presence
and taste blood-crimson seeds
gushing from the pomegranate's core
without gashing the husk.
Let others make the haj
or fall on the sword.
You just need to be more hollow.
Learn to repose in the olive-brown shrine
of this body.
Victorious the mind
that surrenders control.
Give up seeking and dissolve
in the erotic splendor
of the void.
Let your next exhalation
be what pours from the libation cup
offered by a dying warrior.
A death-song swells the throat
in a voice that is yours, and not yours.
Like the curl of smoke from a wick
just blown out, you return
to the lips of the one who says,
"Well done."
Let your next inhalation
be a glittering kiss.
Did no one tell you?
Your breath is the name of God.

BROKEN

A broken commandment
is the open gate
to a wilder meadow.
It may be your sacred duty
to violate the rules.
I smoked an Arturo Fuentes Robusto
with the Bodhisattva.
Asked him if he had any precepts.
He said just one: be healed by your tears.
Then he opened up to me about
his sadness, admitted
he had to come back
because he was lonely.
I said maybe Anthony Bourdain
or Sylvia Plath. He said
maybe Jack Kerouac. I said
all of them wounded one-eyed Buddhas.
My belly was thirsty for repentance
so, I made a bourbon smoothie
and shared it with Jesus.
Asked him if he had any rules.
He said just one: call me brother, not Lord.
Cucumber, mint, and kale
with a shot of Wild Turkey.
Forgive me, it was delicious.
A broken commandment is the open gate
to a deeper rule, unwritten,
harder to disobey.
The laws of the body lead
to the precepts of the soul.
Like the one that says, love anyway.
The one that says, make friends
with the brokenhearted.
The one that says, forgive yourself
again and again... So I discover
the rules I cannot break
by breaking the ones
I can.

ANCIENT JAR

Someone spilled the ancient jar of light.
It can never be stored in the temple again.

Don't drop Dharma in a beggar's cup.
Bottled and sealed, asparagus goes limp.

When you package Yoga at the ashram,
you'd better check the expiration date:

It has to say "Now."
Someone spilled the ancient jar of light.

The vitamin of God dissolves in silence,
but only nourishes your body in action.

It can never be stored in the temple again.
For every breath you take, give one to the poor.

And who are the poor? Look around you.
Everyone is poor.

Someone spilled the ancient jar of light.
Each pair of eyes is thirsty for your glance.

Your smile is nectar, it needs to be shared.
It can never be stored in the temple again.

A Mother doesn't get hungry.
Her breasts are busy with milk and lips.

Someone spilled the ancient jar of light.
It can never be stored in the temple again.

THE FINAL BODY

Inside your body
there's a body made of breath.
Inside that body
there's a fountain of moonlight.
And inside this, a dangling
necklace of woken pearls,
eyes spilling all the worlds they see
down your backbone
with the sound of mountain flowers,
cascade lilies, columbine.
Whoever gave you this breath
used it to weave nests for the stars
singing in bejeweled stillness.
And inside that body
there's one made from ripples
of the void, where you've plunged
into a pollen spore
on the anther of a heartbeat.
And you discover, floating
in that natal sea, a final body
somehow containing them all:
the physiology of space itself,
a luster of silence, secret sheen
of absence in every seed,
so vast and black the Magellanic
Cloud is but a vanishing of sparks
in billows of unknowing.
Drop your concepts,
they won't help you now.
Don't worry, just evaporate.
You'll find your lips and tears again,
made from anti-matter of ecstatic night.
Take off your shoes, take off
the garment of your old story.
Get mud between your toes.

YOU ASKED

When you asked,
How can I face
such a dark world?
the answer was all around you.
The wands of pine
in rain-laden breeze answered,
bell-throated blackbirds
ringing over the wetland
answered, stars
floating on a still pond
answered, dancing
snow of milkweed,
pearl-eyed mushrooms
seeing through midnight
in the forest answered:
This world is not
the seat of sorrow.
This world is sunlight
playing in a risen mist
over the fountain of beauty.
The seat of sorrow is your heart
aching, thirsting
for its own illumination.
But the healing is easy.
Turn your gaze around
and see into your source.
You are that fountain, that
refraction of prism'd beauty.
Listen to the raindrop fall,
how it finds its way home,
as fallen things do,
to the hidden spring
under pungent green moss
where it was born.
Even the raindrop answers,
Yes.

OUR LADY OF THE NURSE LOG

She visits my body as a soft
bolt of lightning in the spine.
Every quark of my gristle sings
to an invisible star about some
incomprehensible connection
between pain and beauty.

Angels cock their heads, perplexed
and ever so sweetly troubled
by the music emitted from my nuclei.
My gravity and grief give them courage.
They long to clothe themselves in bone,
the stuff that weighs me down.

Call her Laniakea,
100,000 clustered galaxies,
my vagus nerve her golden hand,
reaching into flesh.
She lightens and lifts me like
milk-weed on a breeze,
yet she honors my downfall,
laying me in the meadow again,
rooting me wild, nurtured by larvae,
symbiotrophic fungi,
the forgiveness
of ancestral microbes.

You may call her Qi, Prana, Ruuh,
Shekinah Kundalini.
Or let her take the shape of wings
 in dissolving frost.
A drunken worm in the golden apple.
The shadow of a cloud brushing dew
from a faery ring of toadstools.
A hairy caterpillar crawling toward
its rainbow of doom.

Yet I call her the Magdalene,
because I yearn to know her
not as an archetype or abstraction,
but a Person, the way Jesus is a Person,
the way You are a Person, a love
that loves back.

Isn't this the way God plays
in the glistening of human tears?
A single I Am breathed in all bodies,
falling in love with the Self as an Other
again and again, one sap
risen through billions of quivering
stems in a chaos of green?

Beside her I rest on a mossy nurse log
after wandering barefoot all night in the forest.
Listen! There are no words.
I have un-named the fires of heaven.

Only the rustle of death, the growth around us,
sigh of protons, distant quasars arriving,
song of mitochondria, creation's first respiration.
Baby saplings tremble from moldering cedars.
Fir spores ciliate their shakti into loam.
Miryam reaches out her cinnamon foot,
nudging my big toe.

GURU

A teacher fills you.
A guru empties you.
A teacher gives knowledge.
A guru awakens
the knower.
One transmits information.
The other transmits wonder
without words.
Your mind thirsts
for certainty.
Your heart yearns for
breaking open.
If the yearning is intense enough,
the guru could be a cricket.

DOMINION

Take a moment this evening
before you sleep
to remember your death,
your constant companion
on the heartbeat's pilgrim path,
a lifelong friend.
And take a moment each morning
to remember how birthless,
how limitless you are
before the day's first thought.
Recall that you came here
from the kingdom of
gratitude, not want.
How wild and spacious
is the night inside you,
the effervescent vacuum
in every breath, charging
your body with starlight.
How uncharted your green
dominion of beauty,
not the mountaintop,
for it is separate and small,
and nothing grows there.
But the valley, that
generous ever-widening
earthen furrow
where your roots sink deep
and mingle with mine.

TOO EDUCATED

I unplugged my outrage meter
and threw it into the fountain of love.
Next morning a child discovered it
encrusted with emeralds and pearls.
Then the experts arrived.
A professor from NIH proclaimed,
"This is junk science."
A nervous CIA official declared,
"It came from a sunken Nazi submarine."
"Back-engineered alien technology,"
muttered a Pentagon whistle-blower.
"Don't believe a thing you hear!"
said the president of Fox.
But Hafez the bartender gave me better advice:
"If breathing won't clear the clouds away,
assume they're part of the cocktail.
Mix with bitters and orange rind, pour it over
the crushed ice of loneliness."
Then Chung Tzu whispered in my ear:
"If you want to discover a myriad
uses for the useless, abandon every
concept of better and worse.
Be a rose, pollinated by a rogue bull comet,
shouting back at the sky in the lost
language of cocoons."
Easy for you to say, old fellow, but what
do I say? After all, I'm writing this poem!
I say, "Learn to ride the donkey backward
if you want to find the true Way.
Traveling West, gaze Eastward and sing,
follow me, Sunrise! I'll lead you to
Summer orchards, Autumn afternoons.
On Winter evenings I'll show you how
stars are born from sacred darkness."
You laugh? Don't get too educated, friend.
Let's just say there's a fifty-fifty chance
your eyes create the light they see.

CUP

Be a cup
for the grace of the Friend.
Pour and be filled.
Seeking the Master's gaze
or shattering your crown
against those soft brown toes
is not the path.
Lifting the weary,
lighting joy in the broken hearted,
is the wayless work.
Divide your morsel
into miraculous portions,
each more than the whole.
Honor the thirst
as well as the wine,
the hunger in the food.
Take, eat this bread.
Wed your breath.
How near is the Beloved?
The flame of a heartbeat
in your jugular vein.
The task at night is listening
to the vast black bell of silence,
your duty at sunrise,
rejoicing in a sparrow's trill.
Do you know why
Earth spills wild forget-me-nots,
each tiny flower containing the sky?
Because you are awake.
Don't try to understand.
Just be a cup
for the grace of the Friend.
Pour and be filled.

TOO BEAUTIFUL

Too beautiful, the peonies in your garden.
Enjoy them, yet be only half distracted.
Keep a tincture of pure attention stored
under your breastbone.

Don't satisfy this craving right away.
Stay thirsty all night.
Be the vintage flavored
by the darkness that contains you.

Your barrel is hollow, yet this emptiness
imparts a delicate bouquet.
Let your belly growl,
and hunger itself will feed you.

Staunch your lips with no lover's kisses,
and your tongue will sing like a midnight flame.
This journey doesn't end at a teacher's feet;
those sandals are just pebbles on the path.

Compost acquires the scent of roses,
a name the power it names,
and yearning takes on the taste
of what it yearns for.

So, your skeleton assumes
the shape of lightning in the void,
and you become the black hole that your gaze
burns through the master's face.

Only a fertilized yolk, with its spot
of crimson, reads these hieroglyphs
under the dome. What does it mean
to break the egg from within?

It means the whole creation is a wound,
and Jesus can't remember being a grape.
From the beginning, he was the wine
saved for the end of the wedding.

Why take off your shoes
to trample the body of the Goddess,
whose clusters contain moon-blood?
There's a more blessed way to ferment.

Drip into the cask of your own Being.
Stop seeking what is already yours,
and striving to get rid of what isn't.
Don't satisfy this craving right away.

Stay thirsty all night.
Let your longing for the Beloved,
become the Beloved's longing
for you.

KINGDOM

When your Name fell
into my body,
every question in my heart
was answered by one breath,
So'ham.
The distance wasn't great
from the sacrum to the crown.
Why did the journey take
seven times seventy lives?
All I know is,
prayer is the prelude
to meditation,
and meditation is the prelude
to prayer.
There's a kingdom
in my ribs now
whose government is the silence
of a boundless glow,
whose warmth keeps spiraling
around creation like a conch
filled with oceans, wings and sunsets.
When I rest at the center,
I have no enemies.
Everyone I meet is called
the Friend.

THE CHOICE

Can you choose anything
other than what Is?
You think you choose what Will Be,
but when it arrives
it's a pretty strange land.
Of course, you can always choose
what Was.
People make up stories every morning
about last night,
but that's a waste of tomorrow.
There is an imperishable
golden core
in your solar plexus
where happiness does not come or go
like everything else.
The portal to the kingdom
of contentment has never been closed.
Find it in your body, friend.
Just hug the dragon of now.
To welcome this wingéd
ancient fire-breathing moment
with clear eyes, open palms, soft belly
is perfect joy.
To reject it is suffering.
But you can't reject what Is
because you're living it.
So, where's the problem?
Always already free,
this is how a poppy grows.
How a drop of dew dissolves
on a clematis petal.
How a gazelle
offers the pulse of his throat
to the hungry lioness.
Don't worry, we all evanesce
into photons of delight, whirl back
into mothering stars.

LATTE

If you think you are a
"spiritual teacher"
and the lady who fixes your latté
at the drive-through coffee gazebo
is not, then you have
a serious problem.
You too are a student
of the dust mote, the bee
in the delphinium.
Learn to shut up
and smile like a dolphin.
If you say you are an "empath"
and the stray kitten licking
a plastic thimble of half-and-half
beside the trash compactor
is not, then you're seeing
through your I.
Every living creature is an empath.
It's why we're all here.
Even the pilgrim snail
on a hosta leaf feels starlight
that hasn't yet arrived.
Don't you want to touch
the miracle of fur,
the annihilating sweetness
of the hummingbird's tongue,
the bliss-ocean parting for your
slippery dorsal fin?
Then burn away the veil
of mind like a moth wing,
and be the flame itself.

LIFE COACH

A life-coach told me,
"you're perfect right now."
So I tried it, but it bored me.
God is already God,
but who would be Me
if I didn't fuck up
in my own peculiar way?
My blemishes define me.
Jagged edges are the letters
of my true name. Call me
Broken Buddha, Half-Awake.
Breathlessly Creator waits
to see how I sin, completing
her crazy creation.
I am more priceless in the mud,
a ruby uncut, mistaken
for a fallen berry.
What is the sign of my progress?
I'm even less perfect
than I was yesterday.
Dear, I dedicate this poem
to you, the hot mess of your body
on the kitchen floor,
slobbering tears into the linoleum,
Good Morning America
bleeding out in the living room.
I honor the catastrophe
of your hair, your crow's feet,
droop of udder destruction,
the spreading warmth of your
wounded smile in the compost
of uprooted plans and scattered
possibilities, when you finally realize
that no matter how deeply you fall
you are caught, you have plunged
into the hug that was always
already here.

SAVIOR

Olive-skinned Semitic Jesus. Black Jesus from the source of the Nile. Red-haired bumpkin Jesus, poet of waterfalls and cedar'd hills. Jesus the king. Jesus the slave. Jesus the Rabbi who studies with Essenes in Egypt. Jesus the Yogi who visits Kashmir. Jesus the unlettered fisherman. Monastic Jesus fasting for a vision in the wilderness. Jesus mystic bridegroom of Miryam. Marxist Jesus shouting at the rich. Jesus High Priest offering blood sacrifice. Shaman Jesus mixing his spittle with mud as a healing balm for the eyes of the blind. Jesus the lion of Judah. Jesus paschal lamb. Jesus dove. Jesus feathered serpent visiting the Choco rain forest of Ecuador. Non-binary Jesus. Infant Jesus. Jesus who proclaims, I Am, awakening I Am in you. Jesus the Christ whose race doesn't matter, whose gender doesn't matter, who pervades all forms with pure compassion. Jesus the ineffable ocean of silence between your thoughts. Jesus who embodies the cosmos in the hologram of your body. Jesus suffusing every neuron in your brain, every cell of your heart, with Being, Consciousness, and Bliss.

SCENTLESS

The scentless nectar in the rose,
The hollow of the heart that knows,
The emptiness inside the drum
Where rhythms of the dance come from,
The choice of what note not to play,
The space around a star,
The yearning silence that would say
"Beloved" were there any way
To speak of who you are.

HOW SHE WORKS

This is how She works in you.
Beneath the titanium veneer
of patriarchy-orthodoxy-hierarchy,
She weaves dark atavistic roots
into your body.
Her business is entanglement.
You know your chromosomes are braided
with hers, like black shining hair,
when you pass through a portal
of Aloneness into All.
You will never gather her complete
collected works, only shreds
of lost broken scrolls, half-glimpsed
intuitions, after-images
of flame extinguished in
radiant darkness, secret longings
of a tongue for the Spirit
and the Spirit for a tongue,
the pang and purity of each desire.
This is how She works.
She yearns to inflame what is hidden
in the soft tissue of your soul,
that labyrinth of neurons,
the golden scripture of illegible fire.
Your flesh is her Newest Testament.
You are not like any other book,
having fallen directly from the mouth
of the Goddess, spittle into clay,
a loamy tincture anointing the Single Eye
of Jesus, the one he uses to see her.
Do not expect her moon-phases
to repeat themselves.
She'd rather you drown in the apocalypse
of an ancient now.

Her past is not a story,
but the memory of stillness.
She tallies no ledger, no profits
on one page, debts on the other.
Her receipt is the wind.
She beckons you into the desert,
makes your spine a pillar of silence.
This is how She works.
Her revelation a network of mushrooms
spreading ointment while others sleep.
A hummingbird lost in a sip of phlox.
A wolf pack hungry for raw metaphors.
A barn owl dropping the heart
of a mouse down her owlet's gullet.
The belly-rending howl of mother coyote
centering the night.
Burrowed in alfalfa, delighting in fur.
So many places to make love.
Anger just one flavor of fire.
So many whispers in her name.
Her nakedness feral, lethal, lovely,
reveling in slivers, shards
stained with the ichor of wisdom,
the wine of solitude.
And this is how we weave her again,
by the work of remembering,
recalling ourselves
through the fragments we are.

THE TAVERN OF AWAKENING

I got bored with spiritual practices.
Inhale counting 5, hold counting 3, exhale 7.
This isn't prayer, its arithmetic.
Why not just dive into Zero?
I can't lie in Corpse Asana two minutes
without getting anxious about tomorrow.
Is there a Coyote posture, a Wounded Raven pose?
That bronze yogini in her bikini's
been sitting in Full Lotus over an hour.
She's still smiling: did she get a better mantra?
On your inbreath think, "breathing in,"
on your outbreath, "breathing out,"
but why not think, "My grandmother rides her tricycle
through golden atoms of intergalactic chicken broth?"
I took these complaints to the Master,
who just laughed and said, "When did you
actually see me doing any of this crap?"
Then he threw his arm over my shoulder
and led me to the Tavern of Awakening,
where everyone gets instantly drunk
by practicing absolutely nothing.
Nobody knows who's giving the party, or why.
Lovers just show up with big empty cups
and dance in a mambo line all night,
swigging from a jug of stars whose light
won't arrive for a thousand years.
Just before dawn, he whispers in my ear,
"Don't call me Master anymore, call me Friend."
Then he gives me all the advice I'll ever need, for free.
"Honor your body, it's a garden of ancient weddings.
Christ kisses Magdalene here, where your rib is missing.
Be a flute at Krishna's lips, he'll breathe music through you.
And when you bow, bow to your own heart:
its pulse is the hum inside all names of God.
Now take off your shoes, walk softly over the earth,
and pulverize diamonds with your whirling."

KNEAD

Risk being kneaded,
pressed and pummeled
by a heartbeat.
The yeast is sensation.
Taste Aphrodite's nipple in a blackberry.
Pluck Christ from the twig
on a forest trail.
Attain satori through the fragrance
of jasmine, the sound
of a raindrop, atavistic light
from an extinct star
spurting through the tip of a neuron
in the flicker of this idea.
Traveler, it's time
not to believe, but to arrive.
Jesus didn't say to the hungry,
"This is my soul."
He said, "Take, eat, this is my body."
Brown fingers ply the corn flour
into a tortilla.
Your sunburnt shoulder
shrugs off the bathing suit strap.
We're one warmth glowing
in two embers.
Gravity thickens like the Milky Way,
folds her amber batter of distances
into loaves who risk kneading.
Every crumb
of our swirling selves
flavored with the un-created.
Don't cling, don't stick to the pan.
Just savor the essential oils.
The ghee.

WEDDING

Who can say whether
this wedding
was arranged
by the star people,
or by your own
pilgrim heart long before
our grandmothers were born?
All we know for sure
is this,
the minister,
the prayer shawl,
the loving cup,
the maid of honor
winsomely gazing
at the best man,
the canopy of tough
entangled vines,
the gentle flower girls
scattering wisteria,
even the bride and groom
dissolve, dissolve
into the swirling fire
of "I Do."
Tonight, these grapes
become wine.

NEW EARTH

"Behold, I create new heavens and a new earth." ~Isaiah 65

"The kingdom is already spread over the earth, and men do not see it."
~Gnostic Gospel of Thomas, 113

The colossal mistake is to define my existence before I taste it, separating the mind from the world, trapping my thoughts in a loop of running commentary, a fruitless shadow-land, where I merely parallel my body without actually inhabiting it. In such a ghost-world, ideology colonizes the organic, making empathy impossible, and I am in exile, wandering through a shadow-land of abstractions, generalities, and beliefs. Now let me make the pilgrimage back to this moment, this body, this breath. I thirst for awareness, straight, no chaser! Let me inhabit the real, and not the mind's description of it. Let me savor transcendence in the smell of pine, croak of tree frog, outrage of sweet peas clambering through the ribs of a junkyard Chevy. Let me dwell in the wilderness of unmitigated flavor, where the tincture of sensation dissolves my soul, beyond thought. I would be a faithful citizen in the Kingdom of Unknowing, where the ineffable cosmos implodes into ever more edgeless selves, each infinitesimally enfolding the whole.

NOT SO BAD

What does my Guru do?
He's like a doctor.
He looks me over
and shakes his head
to confirm what I've
suspected all along.

You've gone crazy, he says.
Is there any hope? I ask.

I'm afraid your madness
is terminal.
There's nothing I can do
but make you comfortable
until you dissolve.

We sit in silence
for a long long time.

Then he says:
It's not so bad.
Look at me.
I went crazy years ago.
Now, whenever I smile,
thousands of people
sing to me
and give me flowers.

TEN THOUSAND WAYS TO PRAY

Smiling we know is a form of meditation.
Weeping is also prayer.
Worry is beseeching the Whirler of All
to bring you the things you don't want.
Anger is just one flavor of fire.
There are so many ways to become who you are.
To practice the purest tantra in your belly,
digest despair like bacon without naming it.
When the fire of outrage burns a hole
through your forehead, this is profound samadhi.
Now be the hole, fall through it, all the way down
to your rectum. This is yoga.
There are ten thousand ways to pray.
Lying here awake at 3 A.M. is one of them.
Glittering constellations conspire to sabotage clear thinking.
Big-breasted crone moon throbs, making
everyone crazy, then veils herself in raven feathers.
When your planets are ajar, rejoice in darkness.
When your horoscope feels like the web of a spider
who fell into a Starbuck's Frappuccino and got
hammered on caffein, so what?
Rebel empaths invent their own Qigong.
Wrestle with a mud-caked doodle of dubious pedigree.
Practice eye-gaze with your cat, shamanic totem
for the God of Uncertainty. Use holy violence
to defend hen's eggs from a Norway rat.
Breathe the people you hate in and out of your solar plexus
until you distil them into tonic, 200 Proof.
Notice thrown-out alter flowers
on a rainy Monday morning sidewalk.
Don't look away from the porcelain silence
on your mother's face as she takes her last breath.
Wake down. Compost your curses and tears.
Plummet into your belly button tenderly
grieving, sighing, murmuring
"Yes" to the night.

ON THE WAY TO COLD MOUNTAIN

Han Sh'an lived on cold mountain
in the realm of the swirling clouds.
From his hut he could gaze into the universe.
Even at night when the fire was out,
his little room was filled with golden stars.
In summer he watched dandelions grow
among the rocks by his doorway.
In winter he watched snowflakes fall
where dandelions once grew.
Neither the dandelions nor the snowflakes lasted long,
nor had they any meaning whatsoever.
Therefore Han Sh'an found them quite beautiful.
A visitor might bring some green tea,
or a gourd of rice wine.
On his tiny stove Han Sh'an brewed the tea
and whisked it in a white bowl intricately patterned
with healed cracks.
Han Sh'an loved to look into the bowl,
especially when it was empty.
Sipping tea while the visitor told his tale,
Han Sh'an kept silence.
Friend, is the work you do more important
than Han Sh'an's deep listening?
Once, Han Sh'an climbed down Cold Mountain,
for he wondered, "Are all the people in the valley
filled with stories of loss and sadness?"
He gave away poems in exchange for
noodles, cucumbers and saki.
Farmers and villagers he found full of joy.
But most of the people travelled
fierce and fast from city to city.
Their souls ricocheted from each other's
stone faces and fell into the road.
Han Sh'an always noticed such small
fallen things, because his mind was rooted
in the Useless, freed from all anticipation.

He would pick up a lost soul, hold it in
his palm, and breathe upon it, to cool it off.
The soul was like a dusty pearl
far from its oyster bed in the sea.
He would follow a stranger and say,
"Wait, I have your soul, would you like it back?"
And the stranger would turn and stare
at Han Sh'an from the holes in his face,
replying, "Go away, old beggar!"
So Han Sh'an collected many glowing selves.
He gave them to orphans and wanderers
at the ragged edges of the marketplace,
where the real business is done.
Then he decided to end his journey,
and climb back to the realm of swirling clouds.
That is when I met him
on the path to Cold Mountain.
"You must be Han Sh'an," I said,
"please give me a poem."
Han Sh'an replied, "Just look down at the pebbles
in your path. Look up at the crow
in a dead pine, waiting for a tasty mouse.
Look at the gift of the blue sky
between your thoughts.
This is the poem."

REST STEP

Don't take a walk,
give one.
Look over there.
A marmot leaning
against a boulder
in the mist.
You're here to read
the wordless signs,
the details that lie
in your waylessness.
Barefoot or shod,
pause ever
so briefly as you press
your sole's soft center
to the ground.
Hikers of switch-back trails
call it the rest-step,
a sort of meditation
at the heart of going.
The planet can feel
that lost harmony
of your body and your breath,
caressing the earth yet
never quite arriving.
As you meander
through trillium silence
in the dangled gaze of
columbine on sparkling moss,
be careful not to tread on
creamy drops of paschal flower.
This way, you don't disturb
the marmot at his prayers.

FLEECE

Everybody's selling something.
It's a buyer's market.
But there's one thing you cannot purchase:
the breath of self-abandonment.
here's the difference between
love and business.
What's truly priceless is given
for free.
It's all around you, friend,
like sunlight burnishing
each photon of your bones.
The marketer's mind believes
this exhalation is down-payment
for some 20-carot ecstasy
and inhalation is a lease.
But faith is not a contract.
Meditate without negotiation.
Invest the wealth of dawn and sunset,
expecting no return.
Only the poor in Spirit are blessed.
Just declare bankruptcy
and be done with it.
Never bargain with the Beloved.
If someone led you to believe
you'd get anything in exchange
for the gift of your whole Being,
you've been fleeced.

SWAN

Surely, you've been told
a Goddess flows
through your darkness,
thirsting for love.
Don't seek, be drawn.
Wander and be found.
Learn to age the wine
of your longing
in an empty sepulcher.
Pour it wordlessly
into the cup of desolation.
A blossom doesn't open itself.
Something warm and soft
falls into its ovule
from another world.
You have two centers:
one here, one there.
This breath pierces them both.
Honor that piercing as a gift
and you will become the garden
where thorns blossom
and each cell of flesh
is a nectar grail.
Here the Ham'sa swan descends
from ravenous stars
to settle on still waters
and drink from your heart.
Her song? "I Am She."
Your song? "I Am Thee."
It is called the Mystery
of the Bridal Chamber.
Her wings are your inbreath
and exhalation.
This is why you have a body.

PRIMROSE

Silence of the primrose
furiously blossoming
without a gardener.
Rain turning to snow,
then back to rain,
with no decision or
indecision.
Morning does this,
evening does that.
No creator.
Somehow moon and sun
commingle in diffuse
blue whiteness,
yet no ink, no painter.
And without the slightest assistance
from you, dear friend,
countless sentient beings
become themselves
just as they are!
They choose to act,
or not to,
suffering consequences
and rewards,
all so deeply grateful
to you
for your carefree slumber,
for your dancing, your stillness,
and for not
interfering.

YOUR HAPPINESS

If your happiness needs a reason,
you're out of luck on this planet.
If your joy must be earned, you'll
never know how a crack in the asphalt
nurtures a blossoming weed.

Perfection is a waste of time
because it happened long ago,
scattering this chaos of silken
chances into the dark wind.

Every mistake is a crystal door
that makes unfallen angels want to
visit this place, to sharpen their eyesight
on jagged edges, broken tears.

Sift through smoking shards of heaven,
still warm, stillborn.
Use old stories as kindling for a flesh-fire.
Burn up your pain in a deeper pain,
and arrive right where you are.

Discover a thornbush in the woods
where your lover's bones were picked clean.
Weep choicelessly.

You've been trying too hard to stay sober, friend.
The search for awakening makes you sleepy.
Just watch the galaxy spin between your nipples.
Witness the glittering night behind your eyes.
What you're look for is the lens
through which you see.

You've wept mirrors.
Be the ocean in a tear.
Pour your reflections back
into the fountain of grief.

For 7,000 births you drowned in the milk
of the Mother's name, crying, "Kali Ma!"
Now your heart is finally pierced
by the sword of compassion.
She must have touched you there,
just before dawn in the darkest hour,
when you didn't even know you were praying.

Enter that wound,
the healing chocolate agony
of bittersweet desire,
the flower-surge of yearning
just beneath your breast bone.

Call it a portal, the sacred black hole
where you spin the brilliant creatures
of this world from bewildered
stillness.

When you sleep, rest boldly.
Let this breath, then the next,
be footsteps of unknowing.
It only takes a moment, friend,
to turn each cell of your body
into a golden chalice of fire.

THE BELOVED COMMUNITY

I hear the beloved community
singing praises
through their tears,
a gathering of the shattered,
the failed and wanton ones,
filling their violet emptiness
with gratitude.
They flow out of themselves
into each other,
building a fire at the center
of loss.
It could be a hungry log,
a ravenous trash can,
your broken heart.
The holy community
is not a circle
of the perfect.
The untainted are too whole.
They will not disdain
to be parts.
Yet how will the woundless
give thanks?
Through what lesions
would they sing?
O let us call on the one
who lifts us up
into our fallenness!

SHARE

We share the same dust, the same sun.
Your breath and mine
are born from one quietness
and one dark energy pulses
from our heartbeats.
All that divides us is a thought.
Why cling to the mirage?
The radiance in your diaphragm
contains me, the golden roaring
caged in my ribs contains you.
No path led us here.
No one placed this infinitesimal
bell of silence in your body
between what rises and falls.
You simply hear the unstruck sound
and constellations tremble,
the vacuum between them
grows intimate.
Gaze down the black hole
of one fungal hypha
and behold a galaxy of mushrooms.
This meadow hums with death.
Anemone waves, the pterostigma
on a mayfly's wing,
wind-dance of scarlet poppies
conquering the mind of the warrior
and artist alike, everything
softly perishing.
Our circle has so many fragrant centers
God breaks into tears.
The sparrow need not believe it,
she just sings.
We share the same dust, the same sun.
The work of Beauty is stillness.

NOLE ME TANGERE

"But Jesus said to her, do not touch me, for I have not yet ascended to my Father." ~John 20:17

Whoever wrote these words
was still a pilgrim
searching for dawn.
But you have made friends
with darkness.
You know that Magdalene
is an electric breath of Jesus
flowing through your nostrils,
your throat, your belly, your thighs.
And if you listen, she will tell you
what he really said
that morning in the garden:
Touch me.
Feel the shock
of my sweetness.
I will lift your whole body up
into Love's energy.
As wine mingles fruit
and spirit in one cup,
so my flesh and your longing
are the same grace.
Savor this caress,
for the Lord is not an
out of body experience.
Jesus is a sip
of the burgundy void
from the grail of your breast,
the nectar of crushed stars
in a proton of lymph.
Your nerves
are on fire
with God.

RIVER

First you fight the current.
Then you drown.
Then you float on the river like a husk,
like a dropped petal.
Then you sit on the bank and watch
the river flow by.
Sometimes it is a violent flood,
sometimes a gentle murmur.
Then you are the river.
It moves down your spine from the
mountain spring in your crown
through the forests and
meadows of your skin
to the deep cave of your sacrum,
where it soaks into the earth and
nourishes the seeds of
10,000 sentient creatures.
This river sparkles
with infinitesimal constellations.
Distance is illusion.
Heavenly planets form and dissolve
in a spark between axon and dendrite.
This is the river of death.
This is the river of bliss.
Do not fight its terror and beauty.
Drown, float, witness, mingle.
This is the river of your breath.

THE DAY AFTER VALENTINES

Lonely one, where's your soul mate?
Don't you know that otherness
is a looking glass? Learn to hug
every reflection. See God in Dog,
each tulip and toadstool your paramour,
the grizzled stranger hunkered on
the sidewalk your long-lost cousin,
his countenance a treasury of golden
freckles bequeathed to your children.
Put your tears in his cup - salt, not sugar.
Get a crush on the fallen one inside you,
the orphaned shadow of your shame.
Her gaze, I tell you, gives your face
its chiaroscuro: slivers of night
perfecting the glow in your furrows,
your crow's feet, the downcast upbeat
curve of lips that taste world-sorrow.
You dance cheek to cheek with dragons
who turn into angels when you kiss them.
Don't seek your better half:
that's just lack reflecting lack.
50% of you, plus 50% of me
isn't a relationship, it's a pity party
in an antique tear mirror.
Wrap your atoms in angel bling,
pavane with Alcyone of the Pleiades
up the spiral staircase in your spine,
where Cherubim and Furies
from the loam below
tango in the double helix
of beauty and grief
that makes you human.
Whirl, and if anyone asks
who you're dancing with, say
"Dizziness itself!"

VOCATION

When I discovered
the emerald in my chest
I gave up every calling,
wealth, adventure, fame,
just to follow this menial
vocation: I became
a Jewel Polisher.
With the tincture of awareness,
I moisten the soft ragged cloth
of this breath, burnishing
my grail until aloneness
becomes wine.
I drink, and there is plenty.
Let me ever be quenched
by my own thirst.
And when I pray without words,
let the earth, not heaven answer
with a whisper of wild things.
This overflowing emptiness
must be the real name of Jesus.
Surely his body is the morning sun
that brims the mist at the edge the meadow,
clothing my naked eye in Sabbath colors,
umber, olive, wheat. O pilgrim,
keep moving your ragged cloth
over diamond silence,
deeper inside you than your name,
your hope, your story, until
a secret joy outshines the world,
and you taste beyond hesitation
how these marshes and forests,
mountains in their wreathes of cloud,
and even the Beloved's face,
are all one edgeless reflection
of your heart.

ZONE

Why do people keep telling you
to break out of your comfort zone?
Isn't it the sweet spot
where your love comes from?
The more you love, the wider it grows,
that space between heartbeats, until
your comfort zone encircles the stars.
The only thing in heaven and earth
that isn't comfortable is your mind.
The planets never complain,
"I'm stuck in my orbit."
They just keep whirling where they are.
No need to expand your zone.
Expand your astonishment.
Then you'll comprehend how full
of miracles this one square inch
of dirt is, the adventure of whirling
right where you are like the sun,
and hanging without belay
over the cliff of this moment, willing
to drop a thousand feet into another now.
Yet you're caught and held.
A Comforter enfolds you.
On this Summer morning,
why not follow the honeybee
and drown in the pistil of a rose,
at the center of a love without circumference?
Dissolve into a fragrance
that bewilders the whole garden.
Be wilder.
Something infinite invented flowers
to remind you of this soft explosion.
How the pulse of your breath becomes
the motion of repose.
Surely you have wandered into the heart,
and the drunken bee is God,
who keeps stumbling back to tipple
from this wellspring of nectar
in your body.

GREAT STILLNESS

Only through a pilgrimage
do we come to know
that we have always
already arrived.
That the journey from our
lost and far-flung quasar
to the core of the Milky Way
is but a trillionth of a hair's width
sparkling in the synapse
of this thought.
Love asks no image,
but merely to dissolve
the myth of distances.
I think we orbit one another.
You find your center in me,
and mine I find in you.
This kaleidoscopic turning
of all through all
is the Great Stillness.
The glory that swells the East
and melts the West is only
breath-mist, coming and going
on the mirror of mind.
I am a glow that floats about
an inch above your diaphragm.
And when it is soft enough,
your inhalation fathoms my sky,
overflowing the rim of night.
Through pilgrimage you come
to know how earth is healed
by every step, how to massage
the chrism of awareness
into the wounds of God,
root down in the loam
of the ancestor's body,
and embrace my aloneness
as I embrace yours.

TESHUVAH

Why all this talk about Surrender and Return?
You bowed down when you were born.
You came home before the journey began.
Had you not abandoned your soul to darkness,
this dew-sealed morning glory would never
have opened to receive its tongue of fire.
Some naked silence embraced you before
you put on the garment of prayer.

Then the sapphire firmament began to complain
in the language of clouds, your mind, with words
like "commandment," "repentance," "obey."
You forgot that fragrance is a gift, and respiration
is an ecstasy, not a technique.

You no longer leapt on the wine-stained
tabletop of the summer sky.
Your burgundy fled back into the grape.
Discipline locked the gates of joy.
Once you crushed great powers under the weightless
feet of your foolish wisdom, but no more.

You're a shadow made of stone now.
Your gravity is grief, and you think you need
to make some sacrifice. Why not
give up surrender, drop your God-thought,
plunge into the Zero of not believing,
which is a deeper well than waking or sleep,
and even sweeter than a dream of One.

Call it Teshuvah, the ocean of unknowing
globed in a tear: that's where the energy is.
So Jesus commanded the Twelve to do
one thing only: sip from the cup of wonder.
But really, stranger, haven't you always been here,
burnishing this midnight brilliance
with the stillness inside every breath?

LAYAM VRAJA

Don't let anyone market your innocence
and sell it back to you
as a spiritual practice.
Just blow bija bubbles like a baby.
Suck distant galaxies through
your belly button.
Let your intellect plummet
through light-years of surrender.
It's not such a long way into the starry
darkness of your diaphragm,
the space that was here before God said,
"Let there be light."
Rest in the silence before any question
arises: that is the answer.
Thousands of moons ago,
Ashtavakra shouted,
"Layam vraja: dissolve now!"
He was in a cave, and no one heard him.
Yet the rocks trembled, the sky evaporated
into itself, and now we live in the echo.
When the thought of "I" floats by,
we let it pass like a petal on the stream
of abysmal stillness.
Only dreamers take the Night Journey.
Real pilgrims never leave Om.
At dawn, they're still wandering
round and round, truly content
with the shape of zero.
Look at me! Without a word,
I have written 7 million odes to your body.
Without moving, I have visited every star.
On each one, we met
and spoke of love.

MOTHERLAND

In the valley of my backbone
two rivers meet, the Ida and Pingala,
mingling crystal waters of the sun
with emerald waters of the moon.
The gardener is Shakti Magdalena
who comes in the darkest hour,
a temple priestess of the morning star,
to pluck the clusters from entangled
vines of pain and joy. I kiss her
on the lips. This I call breathing.
In her mead-quiet mist, everything
seems motionless, yet dances
in a faint exhalation, laden with
the glow of distant galaxies through
blue vervain and butterfly weed.
All that falls is risen, rain, brackish
desire from wetland lilies, flesh itself,
the marrow of angels lit with fire,
the angry rung bell-beautiful cry
of a great disturbed blue heron.
Earth weeps insouciant poppies, still
foggy with her ambiguous dream.
Where is the path? I follow the ache
of my missing rib. Who comes veiled
in a lapis hijab at sunrise?
My sister the modest sky.
When I pass through the shadows,
she takes my hand to guide me
down a soggy creek bed where
the bones of heaven lie strewn
by an ancient flood of grief.
This is how my body is my soul,
how all that falls is risen, and wherever
I go, my footprints disappear.
No pilgrim can follow my journey.
And when I am most wisely lost,
I become the motherland in whom
all men must find their own way.

BE FOR

Don't tell me
what you are against.
Tell me
what you love.
What you cherish
with your whole body.
Being against
contracts the heart.
Being for
opens the chest
like an orchid
bending toward light.
Now is the time to depart
from the empire of despair
and return
to the palace of beauty,
this human form.
One sweet dark nerve
in your solar plexus
radiates a thousand
times more power
than any opinion.
Let this be your worship
on a Sunday morning.
For a little while,
don't be against anything.
Only be for.
Be for the sun on the table.
Be for the late summer rose.
Be for tears and the laughter
of children.
Wash the whole planet
in the foolishness of God.

SMUDGE

In the birth canal
you were anointed
with the mighty host
of earth's bacteria,
smeared and smudged
with the microbiome.
All tribes shared your blood,
your photons of starlight woven.
Your first breath swirled
the molecules from every race,
ancestral ions, atoms
from the flesh of Jesus,
dust from the skull
of Muhammad, pollen
from the subtle body
of Kwan Yin, lymph
of the first mourner.
Now you need only
one thing more:
touch the stillness
of your Being.
Descend into the hollow
that pulses at the core
of every galaxy,
the uncreated seed
in one atom of your bone.
Rest here.
You will taste
a humble gratitude,
most gentle and quiet.
It will transform you, not
into a luminous cosmic being,
or an ascended being,
but a human being
at last.

LOOK INTO MY TEARS

"Look for the remedy inside the pain, because the rose came from the thorn, and the ruby came from a stone." ~Rumi

Look into my tears.
As every quark carries
some hidden charge
of dark energy,
so every human body
is lit by a secret night.
We don't know its name,
but there's the same ache
in each of us.
We smile to hide it
because we are afraid
it might be ours only.
We never imagine that the mask
smiling back at us
hides the same shadow.
We only find it out
much later, when we look
into each other's weeping.
When we embrace that secret night
in a stranger, and it blossoms,
not because it is forgiven
but because a luminous grace
is the nature of the blackest hour
before dawn,
and a true smile rises
from the heart that stops trying
not to grieve.
Now hear a deeper secret,
a brighter one.
I smile from your face.
You smile from mine.

BREAKFAST AT SHARI'S

Each child   each mother mine   her story
mine   their pilgrim breath   is mine
they cross   my border   I welcome them

all scriptures mine   their wisdom mine
their foolish festivals are mine   all rites
of passage   lead   to my heart

this planet   is my body   rivers my veins
deserts in my hips   oceans my longing
my nerves are ancient   trade routes

every synapse a café   where strangers meet
to share their   fiery wine   when I breathe out
you breathe in   I dream   your dreams

they are mine   I hear your prayers
they are mine   the clusters   you leave
unharvested   at the edge of your vineyard

feed my homeless soul   as the ragged
edges of my meadow   feed yours
the rustle   of my shimmering   barley

helps you sleep   the rain   my gift
to fellow your weeping   in the dark

my voice   to heal you   for I
was wounded too   and healed
by my own singing   which is why

I chant   this prayer   over breakfast
at Shari's Restaurant   and Pie Kitchen
where the waitress   is named Rita

who says   just holler   if you need me
I do   I need you Rita   my night my stars
I share with you   the radiance

of the morning   for I am the sun   let me
cover you   with my golden   warmth
let me enter   every photon   of your flesh

we shall respire   each other   inhale each other
expand each other's   heart-beaten sky
for we include   galaxies   the violent supernovae

stain our emptiness   we are entangled   in some
stormy placenta   we are born   of the night
naked   primeval   unschooled at last

our village shaman   a child   we gather
in firelight   to remember the names
of our tribe   Earth Circle   Autumn Wound

Lost Seed in a Hollow Gourd   there is only
fuel for tonight   tomorrow   there will only
be fuel for tomorrow   we believe   in nothing

we believe   in everything   there is never
enough   there is always   enough
for we gaze   into each other   and we see

through a single   Eye   yearning for the sun
we are not   what we see   we are
what sees   we are   the light of the world

TO FLOWER

To flower
out in sunshine and air,
a seed must fall
and bury herself
in the loam,
where the dead gather
like old old friends
to compost her pain
into beauty.
I am a seed. To sing,
I fall into silence.
To radiate golden
joy, I fall
into darkness.
To know wisdom,
I leave the dry land
of thinking
and fall into the ocean
between thoughts.
Are you poor in spirit?
Do you desire
true wealth?
Be a seed.
Vanish into your opposite.
Give thanks for the least,
a blade of grass,
the stillness
of the swallowtail
on a weed,
the rise and fall of
this breath.

HIDDEN WORK

Put some space around
         your story.
      The deepest blue encircles
         every storm.
Why try to stop the whirl
      and chatter of the mind?
         Just stop believing it.
This tale of lack and sorrow
      is time past,
         but the sky
      you hold around it
         is now.
Why not fill the hollow
         in every cell,
      the star-strewn vacuum
         in each atom of bone
with this delicious inhalation?
         What is real?
      An ancient presence.
         A pulsing stillness.
      The honey of silence,
            sweet sticky abyss.
Drown here
      in a secret well
         between your breasts.
      Do it while you're still
         on earth.
This hidden work
      replenishes the soil
         and suckles
            one breath
      in eight billion bodies.

FOLLOW

Follow the one who leaves
no footprints.
Let the next breath be
your teacher.
Those who stop seeking
are anointed
by a royal Presence.
The silence between
the furious of stars,
the glistening
between your thoughts,
this never slumbers.
Be like the moon tonight,
borrowing splendor
from what is unseen.
I give you a solemn promise.
A path made on water
has no end,
and no beginning.
Take the wayless Way,
and a golden flower will softly
silently explode in your body,
the very motion of your
heart's stillness.
How can I be sure?
I have tasted the honey
of the Master's glance
and I know where it is stored.
In you, my friend.
In you.

SOMMELIER

Under yellow yeast dust, a husk.
Under the husk, a rind.
Finally the sweetmeat, only then
the nectar, luscious alone.
I am telling about your heart.
Not just the quivering organ
thirsty for your next inhalation,
but all its interior sheathes
of serum and amrita.
Only one who tastes the juice
inside can point deeper, whispering,
"Open. Penetrate. Crush."
You would never in a thousand
years have run your tongue
around a plum.
Bitten into pomegranate.
Even the apple skin
would have repelled you,
metallic and tasteless, like kissing
the chrome on a car.
The pith itself a golden window
pulverized by hunger.
You might have turned from all
earth's bitterness and beating,
this muscle and cruor.
Doubtful you'd have ever torn
the veil away to savor a grape,
this orb of liqueur.
Which is why you need a sommelier
to slash the flagon of your chest,
a guide to the fragrance of the terrible
sweetness within, and what is inside
even that, the sparkling wine
that surges through blackness,
a fountain of stars
after you've used up
all your breath and blood.

TOUCHED

Better than
a thousand hours
of disciplined sitting
are seven breaths
of effortless meditation,
three steps
walking barefoot
in the garden of gratitude,
one moment
of adoration
in the secret chamber
of the heart,
if you have been touched
by the madness
of Grace.

MARRIAGE SONNET

Helpmate, sister, friend, O paramour!
What passes is not time, but our attention
to the wedded graces we came for:
freedom to remark, or not to mention
forgotten promises; without a word
to keep our half, or choose forgetting;
share the wonder of a hummingbird,
the passion kindled by a setting
sun over the distant golden hills,
this orchid from a thoughtful daughter
bursting its purple plenty, how it spills
a loving cup of Lethe-water,
how we drink of it, grow young at last,
not with regret for all that is stillborn,
nor yearning for a scent of rose in thorn,
but tasting full the presence, with the past.

GENESIS

As you fall asleep tonight,
keep falling.
Fall into star-foam.
Play in the wave-nature
of silence.
Rise up, slide down
the pearl moonbeam
of every breath.
Drift over phosphorescent
swells of Turiya,
beyond slumber your sail
billowing *So'ham*.
Sink into a froth of worlds
unborn,
infinite possibility
on the tip of your nose.
No higher, no lower,
no matter or spirit.
Go where birth and death
have not yet been divided z
into time.
What rudder, what hand,
passing through such
un-created waters,
could cleave the formless
from the void,
Tohu from *Bohu*?
Surrender
is the subtlest art
because it happens
without you.
Now witness your waking.
This is the first morning.
Who passes seamlessly
from the dream of night
to the dream of day
never sleeps.

INVENTORY OF CIRCULAR THINGS

Be the roundness in
whatever spins.
Don't look for any center.
The shape of your sit-bone
saddled in the space
between the sun and moon.
A pebble honed by eons of water,
the way your embryo was
rounded by swirls of desire.
Centripetal design of the nest
in the mind of the song thrush
even before the sky is
curved into an egg.
A proton reeling in its star,
yet letting out light-years
of slack.
How a withered dandelion
with nothing left to give
disperses her useless beauty
in silver filaments,
inspiring the galaxy.
A new moon's rim of emptiness
storing up the ocean's pulse.
Or the shape of your journey
exerting its circumference
of wonder
from belly to horizon.
Notice also the implicit
prayer bead haloing every stranger.
Claim it as your tear.

SECRET

There's a secret in our madness.
Everything is spiritual.
This mossy rock the garden
of paradise.
A toadstool made of God.
If you look close up,
the wing of a fly is scripture.
Your inhalation the Creator's
most intimate name.
A fistful of fur on the miniature
golden poodle
infested with celestial beings,
countless as stars.
Pilgrim, didn't you know?
There's a secret in our madness.
Everything is holy.
The radiance of your destination
permeates the place where you began,
and the space between them
is one breath of grace,
a distance from the forehead
to the chest.
All that prevents
supreme attainment
is seeking.
Caress the earth with your footsteps
like one who buffs a chalice.
What does it mean to whirl?
It means to give up the path
and dance in all directions
at once.

AQUIFER

"Aquifer" is my favorite word.
The upper half of her body
is the sound of water,
the lower half the sound
of fire,
like a despondent moonbeam
throwing herself into
a dewdrop
deep in the forest.
Now the aquifer is underground,
but spoken it rises
through my lips, a breath
emerging as a woman entirely
carved of pearl and amber;
or an undulating mist, merely
eerie and wise, Sophia
permeating every form of
pain and sorrow, softening
the stone, weaving
a mouse nest out of moss
in a fallen helmet.
Less illusory than I am
to myself, her wild athyrium
greening the planet, now
a wellspring, now a cloud
ridden by a mountain,
now snow, then rain, now loam,
and inside loam, the river
of forgetting that awakens
an earthworm.

THE GARDEN WHERE NOTHING WENT WRONG

*I found this poem, part of the lost version of Genesis, scrawled in weeping
Proto-Sumerian runes on limestone walls in the cavern of my rib cage.*

This sense that something
went wrong.
The sense that we have fallen
and taken the world down with us.
The sense that all
might have turned out better
had we not made some
colossal mistake in the beginning.
The sense that nature
disapproves, and every
flower is shouting
about the impending cataclysm,
because a dark mother
tasted the fruit of unbearable joy.
Dear friend, don't you know
that humans hesitate and cower
before uncertainty, age after age,
inventing the same story?
It's the way we feel when we
don't know how to breathe,
when we don't know how to
pause between our thoughts,
to savor the delicate bouquet
of this moment.
Some say heaven will appear
when this tribulation is over.
I say heaven is an infinitesimal
grain of silence
at the tip of your exhalation,
just before you receive
the gift of your next breath.
Meet me here.

We'll dance barefoot
in the garden where nothing
ever went wrong.
Our vines of desolation
will explode into wine.
We'll crush the dark cluster
of bittersweet wanting
into a radiant downpour,
drowning fear and hope
in golden outrageous joy.
Let's return to the wilderness
where there was only one tree,
rooted deep in our own
groundlessness,
its branches bending low,
laden with ripe sweet worlds,
a sparkling serpent uncoiling
from its living seed,
spiraling up the very spine
of the Goddess.
Where was that Eden, really?
The serpent was Wisdom.
The Goddess was Eve.
She marveled at the dust
in the palm of her hand,
blew upon it,
and created a Man.

PERFECT MORNING

Isn't this is a perfect morning
to bow before your body?
A perfect morning to
touch your foot and say,
"Forgive me, I'm sorry."
Isn't this a perfect morning
to caress your heart with
a feathered breath,
and love who you already are
instead of who you must become?
A perfect morning to fix
yourself a cup of tea
and serve it to your own lips?
Perhaps the perfect morning
to wander
into the back yard,
pick yourself a sprig
of blossoming plum and
place it in a vase, a jar will do,
and say, "Why thank you, friend."
When you gaze into that little
spindle of pollen,
doesn't it become the whorl
of a trillion suns, just for you?
Isn't this a perfect morning
to honor yourself
so deeply in the stillness
of your partner's smile
that you become the sky?
Breathe out now.
Let all your enemies disappear
so quietly, so softly,
because they were never there.

HUG

Hug yourself like a sleeping cat.
Wake before dawn, inhale
the morning star into your lungs,
rain scent of alfalfa, the smell
of Presence. Learn from an elk
in the meadow to graze softly
on details, munching clover,
tiny daisies. The secret is to fall
in love with things unnoticed,
neither bought nor sold.
Breathe down to your seed.
Be a dangling chain of bells
in the music of the wind.
If you have wings, use them.
If not, don't pretend.
Let sap flow through
the half-broken branches
where you graft new friends
onto your body.
Never close your wounds.
They become eyes.
Loosen your crown, leave it tender.
Let your naked feet be bruised,
walking slowly over the bones
of paradise, not
like a landlord
but a pilgrim.

RATIO

"He who sees the Infinite in all things, sees God. He who sees the Ratio only, sees himself only... I will not reason and compare: my business is to create."
~William Blake.

You fail only by comparison.
To whom? To what?
Suns do not mutter,
"Which of us is brighter?"
Undiminished by a ratio
of otherness, you are ensouled,
not by a fraction, but a singularity.
Your face was already beautiful
before those fair eyes fell
into this world of aberrant
refracted beams, and these
flesh atoms from the first
breath of creation arranged
themselves into a brief wild
all-mirroring symmetry.
Now is the time to repose
in your own peculiar light.
Cultivate stillness by dancing,
by swaying ever more gently
toward your center.
Cultivate silence by singing
more softly, until only
your nerves can hear you.
By letting a thousand thoughts
swirl like dust in a sunbeam,
attain perfect emptiness.
By allowing weeds to blossom,
cultivate exotic flowers. Name
this fallow meadow, "The Garden."
You've already survived.
You've won, because you are here.
Now just be incomparable.

KENOSIS

"I have become the original Image freed from its reflection...
The chains of my forgetfulness only existed in time...
Now, where time rests in the stillness of Eternity, I repose in silence."
~Gnostic Gospel of Mary, 3rd C.

Mary Magdalene bore his child.
She became pregnant by him.
But Christ did not fill her womb.
He filled her heart, which grew
infinitely round with his image,
like an egg.
She brought the pregnancy to term
by emptying herself,
and became a mirror to reflect
the Beloved, accomplishing
this secret work of yearning through
the fertility of silence, and the deep
companionship of solitude.
Thus, Mary gave birth to her own anointing.
She exchanged a life of hollow things
for living no-thing full of bliss, and whole.
You too are a Magdalene
walking on waves of the Moon Path,
keeper of the Sun's likeness.
You too enfold the luminous egg,
the round and silent work
of mystic motherhood.
It is no small accomplishment of your shadow
to give birth to the radiance of Christ.
Hidden beams from your conception
penetrate all other souls.
Each of us is a hungry mirror,
yearning for reflection, longing to contain,
by means of our emptiness,
the beauty of each other's face.

YOU ARE HERE

Those pictures of the galaxy that point
to a tiny dot and say, "You are here!"
They are mistaken.
The Milky Way is inside.
You are the space that holds
every *bindhu* and *ayin soph*,
every dot and point of view.
Breath flows down through your sacrum
into the planetary core,
then up to your crown, gently,
briefly dissolving
in the blue sky above.
Touch the moon, then the sun
with a silken ray of pure attention.
It will lead you to the radiance
you came from,
to which you will return,
bearing the fruit of lifetimes.
Those stars are not as far off as you think.
It is your thinking that distanced them.
They're not strangers, but ancient friends,
pilgrims within. Now greet them
in your body with a holy kiss.
The glistening filament of your prayer
threads jewels of amazement
through your vertebrae,
worlds of possibility and
miracles of healing,
which only happen because each pearl
is hollow, and it is the hollow
in the pearl
that makes you whole.

SOLSTICE

Today is slightly longer
than yesterday or tomorrow.
So what?
The earth is wobbly.
Somewhere a stray kitten
is shivering in summer rain.
Somewhere a neglected boy is
loading his father's gun.
And a mother flees across the river
ever Northward in search
of a home for her child.
This inhalation could be a summer solstice,
this exhalation a winter one.
So what if Mercury's in retrograde?
You are not your horoscope,
you are the sky.
So what if the Lion and Bull,
the Ram and Scorpion cross horns,
their fangs and stingers
in outrageous combat?
They'll come down at dawn to drink
from the silent oasis
of your waking.
You are not that riot
of ancient fires and distant sparks.
You are the largesse of immemorial darkness
through which they glitter, rear, and clash,
stagger back, and wander on.
If there is a God, she doesn't care
so much about your stars
as she cares about the smile you could have
shared with a friend last night,
the grace you might say to a stranger
this evening, the breath you could savor
this very moment,
like a sunrise in your chest.

PAY ATTENTION

*'Ano raniyan, mahato mahiyan: smaller than the smallest,
greater than the greatest." ~Katha Upanishad*

Pay attention to the mystery
of little things,
how least creatures burst
with wild sweetness.
A crumb
fallen from the alter, stuck
to the janitor's boot-sole
is also the body of God.
A single breath
descending, ascending
through your trachea
contains the whole story
of salvation.
Yesterday's flowers
that arrived too late,
still unwatered.
In the greenbelt between condos,
mysterious deer trails
spiraling into themselves,
wilderness even here!
The scent of three unpicked
Autumn tomatoes,
glowing hollow lanterns
full of the moon.
Notice the spider
flinging her silken path
from a garden Buddha
to the withered rose.
How the last evening light
like the hand of the dying
fondles very small objects,
not with regret
but inextinguishable gratitude.

BECOME KINTSUGI?

Sometimes I cry, but these are not
my tears, they are tears with no eye.
Tears of the moon, tears of September.
Of the vine maple, the crow,
a staggering elk with ruined antlers,
gray raindrops of the mountain
pouring through the soul and soil
of my body.

It is a time for letting petals go
and the last berry, time
to settle and lean bare
against the unpainted barn
like an old hoe,
like a listening heart
leaning on the comfort
of approaching darkness
in silence after evensong.

Don't explain this, how beauty
is so much like sorrow,
my grandmother's brown vase,
its silken cracks shaped
like a vast bolt of lightning.
Perhaps I should restore it
with burning liquid gold.
Become kintsugi?

Or rest my gaze upon a poplar leaf
on the useless bench in my garden,
one of myriad fallen things
in a brittle season rich with
gilded offerings, tears of time,
pouring through the soul and soil
of my body.
Tears with no I.

BUT NOT ME

My body's getting old, but not me.
Each night before I go to sleep
I take out my eyes, wipe them
with a tissue and set them on
a table by the window where
they can absorb moonlight.
I unsnap my ears and balance them
against each other. To the eyes,
lying beside them, they look like
delicate mollusks holding oceans
of silence which I carefully pour
into a thimble, and sip. Then I
unpeel my lips very slowly
to avoid the pain, folding them
in a crescent smile by my pillow,
where I can reach them if a nightmare
needs to shout, or just to weep.
It is not the tears that matter
so much as the sound, the name
you try to say when you are crying.
I remove most of my fingers, toes,
other body parts, unscrew them.
They fall so wistfully on the oriental
which belonged to my grandmother.
And you are here beside me. We have
our breath, that cannot be taken from
our spirit. We have hearts that cannot
be taken from the rhythmic beating
of our souls, two moths at one candle.
What's left, my dear, my partner, lover,
friend? The stars, which are also parts
of this body. And the sky at night.
And all that does not sleep.

MYSTERY OF THE MAGDALEN

To enter the mystery of the Magdalene is to enter the mystery of healing. To enter the mystery of healing is to enter the numbest of our bones, the places most discomfited. Here is a deeper mystery: to heal our own marrow is to heal the earth. Are there not grottos in your body where you meet the Magdalene gazing into her candle of solitude? She might not attend the yoga retreat in Bali, the ashram at Big Sur. She might not appear white-robed in lotus pose before 10,000 chanting devotees. She falls dustward in teardrops, spilling from a broken half-moon onto the rubble of ruined condominiums in Ukraine. She flows through lead water pipes of underground Detroit, wades across the Rio Grande, clutching someone's baby, praying not to be sent back. And don't imagine that she seeks justice, for justice is not enough. Justice divides the righteous from the damned, separates white from black, woman from man. Justice is in love with blame. But Mary holds us all accountable for everything, bearing in her flesh the wounds of each, the microbe, the Messiah. She is the salt of compassion in the weeping of those who lose hope. She feeds the green in our darkness. And in her gentlest breath, she offers the Beloved all the pain we cannot carry.

COME TO PASS

I did not come to get angry.
I did not come to be sad.
I did not come to brandish
a skeleton of worn-out stories
under my skin.
I came to find a forest place,
the glade of moonlight we only
discover when we're lost,
where animal guides gather to dance,
and ice crystals sparkle with the silent
echo of next Spring's flowers
I came to feel the waves of peace
that swell from the grief ocean,
and to fail in every endeavor
where I might have imagined
myself in control, until I learned
that never touching bottom
is called "the heart."
A lover waits, ever longing for me
to plunge into myself
like a dagger of absence,
a diamond blade that hones what is
with the brilliance of what is not.
We shall sit on the bank and watch
the streaming of the world,
and it shall come to pass.
Do not call me irresponsible, I respond
to mothwing, gong of raindrop,
purple thistle-touch of evening,
threnody of grandma raven
just as she dissolves in Winter mist.
Friend, if you want an answer, sit with me
where there is no question.
Drink a little more passionately
from something nameless that flows
through the darkening meadow
of this moment.

I ASKED LOVE

I asked Love to guide me
and Love said, "I don't want you
to go anywhere."

I asked to see the face of the Beloved.
Love turned her shining absence
into a looking glass.

Love said, "Awareness of Awareness
is better than a thousand
mountain tops."

So I gazed into my Being until
the light became too bright
for any self at all.

My darkness was a sheath
for Shiva's blade,
for Shakti's breath of fire.

Still I asked Love to bear me
up to the diamond peak
on mystic wings.

Love said, "Bow down.
Plunge your nostrils into compost,
humus and sod."

And that is how I came to be
the guest of honor
at this feast of worms.

IDENTITY

I am not a tribe, I am not a color,
I am not a gender or a class.
I am a Person.
And there will never be another I
in all the fallen uncreated stars.
No genus contains me.
No species explains me.
I am all energy and every byte
of information configured in one
instant fragile twist of the kaleidoscope,
the sparkle of a perishing mosaic
in the crystal pandemonium of the Goddess.
Earth did not need another Buddha.
Earth did not need another Jesus.
She needed Me.
My piercing love note shall not
be likened or heard again.
A diamond of dew on Indra's web
reflecting every entangled jewel
as each reflects the all-woven, I globe
the cosmos in a drop, encircling the sea.
I am the singularity.
I am billions, a hologram of human faces,
yours in mine, as mine in yours.
We are each other's eyes.
We both embody paradise
enfolding super-clustered intergalactic fire,
incorporating gemstone, flower,
fungal spore, each pilgrim thing
of four legs, fin or fur, of stained-glass wing
or cilia that root our DNA in cedar sap,
tse tse fly larvae, loam demons
of the mycorrhizal network,
basso continuo hum of the microbiome.
Yet still inviolable, unique, I am who Am,
as you are unique and inviolable.
I am a Person.

ANCIENT BOW

I was lit by a flame. My spine
is a wick in the candle of this body.
Years ago, naive and foolish,
I sat each morning and evening
in meditation. For in those days,
I thought I needed the grace
of the Teacher. Childlike,
I believed that his whisper might
free my mind and open my heart.
Now I have grown old, and many
years have passed. Guess what?
I am still naïve, still thirsting
for my Teacher's grace,
each morning and evening
still sitting. And his whisper
has become the silence in my mind,
his face a frolic of golden rays
in the sweet desolation of my rib cage.
And still I bow, and when I bow,
I'm every bow that ever bowed,
ripples in an atavistic stream,
the River of the First Genuflection,
flowing back to the beginning,
where the Sun pays obeisance
to the motherhood of Night.
This lamp did not light itself.
A fiery Otherness touched me.
Now tell me, is this flame that
annihilates my heart yours or mine?
All I know is, souls are passed
from wick to wick, and we are all
kindled by an ancient gratitude.
I am a holocaust of moths
dancing too near the candle.

EASTER MESSAGE FROM ISSA

Savor your breath, it is my Holy Spirit:
this is the anointing of the Christ.
While still on earth, taste each photon of your flesh
as infinite light: this is my Resurrection.
Welcome all into the radiance that shines
from your chest: this is my Kingdom.
Crucify my otherness, glorify me as your Self,
for suffering is clinging
to an ever-perishing outward form.
Be risen from the tomb of the past
into the garden of this moment.
I taught this simple Gospel before entering
eternal *samadhi* as your very Presence.
What does it mean to say that I am risen,
ascended to the right hand of God?
It means, I have become
the silent Witness within you.
Feel my compassion as your own true nature.
Have a joyful feast, share everything.
Billions of years ago, this Easter feast began
when the Breath of Creation offered the stars,
the galaxies, garlands of galaxies, to her Beloved.
In silent worship He witnessed her whirling,
for He is the wonder and She is the dance.
In her dance, She offered you, before
you were conceived, a trembling flame
in the mirror of his love.
Who told you about "original sin?"
You were whole, you were divine, you were
a perfect oblation before the sun and moon were lit.
And still with every inhalation you are washed in beauty.
Then why did that mothering Breath make offerings:
a hyacinth, a host of stars, your embryo, a tear?
So that Love could taste the Beloved in each creature.
The cosmos is not an atonement, but a feast.
Have a joyful celebration, share everything.

106

JUST FOR TODAY

"My soul is exceeding sorrowful, even unto death:
stay here and watch with me." ~Matthew 26:38

Just for today,
a Sabbath from knowledge.
Who knows?
Just for today,
a Sabbath from judgment.
Forgiveness is your nature.
Just for today, A Sabbath
from being right.
If a day is too long,
Then just for one hour?
If an hour is too long, then
just for one breath?
Even that is enough
to bathe a thousand stars
with your love.
Just for a moment, friend,
Stay with me.

SPILL UP

Snap off the spires.
Break the hierarchy
of skyscrapers
into kindling.
Throw it on smoldering coals.
Around the fire,
make a murmuring circle
that needs no leader.
Remember where flowers come from.
Root down in what you've forgotten,
what you might become,
cilia tangled in sacred soil.
Do it in darkness
while the birds are still asleep.
Walk barefoot on mossy stones,
keeping your balance with
empty hands and arms outheld.
Close your eyes, imagine
nothing but the night,
as water sings beneath you
in secret caverns.
Feel the mud-suck of gravity
like a meditation.
Germinate, swell, burst open.
Spill up
into the sky
those crinkled rainbows
you've been holding too long
between your ribs.
Let it be said of your people,
"They grew in the shadows,
then they danced."

BODY SHAPED LIKE THE WILDERNESS

Just as Christ is in Mary
there is prayer inside this breath.
Someone, yet not another,
watches from within
the weeper.
There is a body
shaped like the wilderness
made of dark matter and fire
inside the soul.

Just as Christ is in Mary,
there is energy in silence.
When evening falls, pulsars
populate the blackness of zero
with countless powers of -1.
She holds up an egg.
Her eyes long to tell us
what she will not say.
Where is her voice?
Where is yours?

Just as Christ is in Mary,
Spring trembles in a bleached femur,
the marrow now burnt umber loam,
undulating larvae, a feast of amoebae.
Within the seed, is there a yearning
greener than green?
Within the egg, is there light?

She will not speak, yet she will intone
a wordless canticle of dust
rising out of the belly
of all things.
A ululation that passes over her tongue
like wind at night without a husband.
Just as Christ is in Mary,
love is burning,
born of aloneness.

THE END

Prepare for the end of time.
Practice the mysterious art
of bewilderment.
Spread your translucent
tear-stained wings
and pulsate at a frequency so fast
it stills you.
This is how you rise into
the kingdom of the hummingbird,
far above the ministry of fear.
This is how you enter
the holographic quantum crystal
of the present moment,
a sphere of gratitude
with no entropy, no mind-leak
into past and future,
which are only thoughts.
Here's the secret: tell everyone!
The end of time is this breath.
Have you shattered the ampule
of your wound-fragrance?
Somewhere in these
petals of fire
there is nectar for the one
who is not afraid of drowning.
Dwell in the uncertain
and call it possibility.
Drink from the unknown
and call it wine.
Savor a silent inhalation
through your broken heart
and call it bread.
This feast is better
than a thousand right answers.

HOMECOMING

How many times
must I hear Buddha say,
"breathe in, breathe out,"
before I can do it myself?
I got tired of being spiritual.
So I came home.
To the place where
my mind and Buddha-mind
are one cerulean sky
wrapped around a robin's egg
in a bold little nest on a lilac tree
by the back porch.
I came home, built a fire,
made strong green tea.
Took out my mother's
bone China cup
and ran my fingers
over the crazing, the lace
of imperfections in all
that once was white.
We're full of cracks
and dark patches, aren't we?
Millions of moist lips
on the verge of a single kiss.
The world feels brown and blue.
I came home to hug you.
Got tired of being spiritual.
Now I'm just
Being.

ONE WORD PRAYER

God has given me
a practice,
the beginning and end
of every path.
Rest the mind
in the heart,
breath scattering stars.
God has given me
a discipline.
Receive just what
the moment brings,
want nothing more,
learning to say,
Enough,
the one-word prayer
of ineffable gratitude.
Here is a secret.
It's not what
God gives me
each moment
that makes me rich,
it is this prayer.

ACKNOWLEDGMENTS

I am grateful to the following journals, both online and in print, that published poems contained in this book:

Monk: Art and the Soul
Tiferet Journal: Fostering Peace through Literature and Art
Braided Way Magazine: Faces and Voices of Spiritual Practice
Science and Nonduality

Some of these poems have also been shared in services and celebrations of the Mythica Community (*www.mythicacommunity.org*). I am very grateful to their founder, KaYleen Asbo, Ph.D., who inspires seekers from all over the world as a Mary Magdalene scholar and pilgrimage leader. Through her spiritual gatherings, I was introduced to the stunning work of our cover artist, Sue Ellen Parkinson, for whose generous creativity I also give humble thanks. (*www.sueellenparkinson.com*)

NOTES: A GLOSSARY

AYIN SOPH: Hebrew, a term from Jewish Kabbala. In Sanskrit, BINDHU. The infinitesimal dot of darkness and no-thing, from which all creation's light and energy pours, originating in the silent center of our own consciousness.

BIJA: Sanskrit, "seed," refers to the most powerful kind of mantra, a single syllable received at initiation, whose subtle sound vibrating in the nervous system can bring awareness to the source of energy and creation, when empowered by grace.

IDA, PINGALA: Two streams of energy, subtle nerve-currents in a meditator's body: the male solar energy and the female lunar energy. They unite in the mystical marriage, twined around the SUSHUMNA, the Tree of Life in the spinal cord: thus the Caduceus of Hermes, derived from India, which became the symbol of Western medicine.

ISSA: A most ancient form of Jesus' name, used especially in India.

KENOSIS: Greek, a word embedded in Philippians, 2:6-11, one of the most ancient Christian hymns. It means, "to empty oneself," as Christ did. One of the original spiritual practices in the primitive Church, quite comparable to the realization of "Sunya," emptiness, in Buddhism.

KINTSUGI: In Japanese pottery, the technique of filling cracks with liquid gold.

MAGDALENE: Mary Magdalene appears throughout these poems. Exploring Medieval pilgrimage routes in Europe, I met her 50 years ago on July 22, her feast day, in Magdalene Priory, a small monastery in Province, built near the cave where she dwelled as a hermit after the resurrection, the West's first Christian mystic. She led me from the mind to the heart. Through her grace, my practice of Advaita Vedic meditation and Christian devotion were fully integrated into one pathless path.

ONE WORD PRAYER: In Orthodox Christian practice, the Jesus Prayer settles into a single word, Jesus, a breath mantra, becoming "one-word prayer," in Greek, "monologisthos eucharistos."

SHAKTI: Sanskrit, "power," Lord Shiva's creative energy and feminine consort. He is the stillness. She is the dance. Without her, no creation. The West calls her "Holy Spirit." In the Bible, "spirit" and "breath" are one word. She who dances the cosmos is the very Spirit in our breath.

SO'HAM, HAM'SA: So'ham is the universal breath-mantra in Yoga tradition, literally meaning, "God I Am." The two syllables express the inner sound vibration of inhale and exhale, or as the poet Kabir called it, "the breath inside the. breath." The Upanishads give this same mantra as "Hamsa," which also means "swan" in Sanskrit.

TESHUVAH: In Judaism, the deepest spiritual practice, repentance, literally "returning" to God.

TOHU BOHU: Hebrew, Genesis 1:2, "formless and void."

TURIYA: Sanskrit, in Vedic philosophy, the "fourth state of consciousness," beyond waking, dreaming, and deep sleep, abode of the Self, pure awareness.

VIRACOCHA: The Incan Creator, most important ancient deity of South America.

ABOUT THE AUTHOR

ALFRED K. LAMOTTE has authored four volumes of poetry with Saint Julian Press. He has co-authored four books of artwork and poetry with artist, earth-steward, and farmer Rashani Réa. His poems have appeared in several journals and anthologies. An interfaith college chaplain, meditation teacher, and instructor in Philosophy and World Religions, he has degrees from Yale University and Princeton Theological Seminary. He lives on the shore of the Salish Sea near Seattle, WA, with his wife Anna and his dear friends, Emerson and Finn, who are four-leggéds of the golden fur. Visit his Amazon author page at: *amazon.com/author/alfredlamotte* and his poetry site, Uradiance, at: *http://yourradiance.blogspot.com.*

Typefaces Used

ALTHEA - Althea
GARAMOND - Garamond
PERPETUA TITLTING MT – LIGHT

Milton Keynes UK
Ingram Content Group UK Ltd.
UKHW050628041223
433752UK00012B/683

9 781955 194211